PRAISE FOR *THE FOUR QUESTIONS*

In *The Four Questions*, Vaisesika Dasa shares with us a treasure of wisdom that is profound, universal, and most importantly, practical. He reveals principles to help us not only overcome daily challenges, but to also connect us to our heart's deepest aspirations.

– **RADHANATH SWAMI**, *New York Times Bestselling Author of*
  The Journey Within *and* The Journey Home, *Spiritual Activist and Founder of Govardhan Eco Village and Annamrita*

Using the timeless wisdom of the Vedas, Vaisesika Dasa offers us a path to transform our lives and reach our highest potential by asking *The Four Questions*. By doing so, we gain a "vision of eternity," as described in the *Bhagavad-gita*. A profound gift to guide us to our highest potential.

– **DR. JAMES R. DOTY**, *New York Times Bestselling Author of* Into
  the Magic Shop, *Professor of Neurosurgery Stanford University, and Founder of the Center for Compassion and Altruism Research and Education*

Vaisesika Dasa has a unique ability to take ancient wisdom and translate it into practical tools for modern life. He does it eloquently in his new book *The Four Questions*.

– **GOPI KALLAYIL**, *Chief AI Business Strategist at Google, Author of*
  A Happy Human, *Board Member of Grameen Foundation, and Advisor to the CEO for Plaeto, Task Human, Jiffy.AI*

These four questions serve as my guides in times of difficulty, relieving the heavy load of expectations that I often place on myself.

– **LIMENG MA**, *Media and Protocol Affairs Specialist,*
  Global Diplomacy Conferences

Vaisesika Dasa proposes four simple, practical questions that can guide readers of any background, nationality, or faith to find purpose, develop quality relationships, and live happier, more fulfilling lives.

– **GIRIRAJA SWAMI**, *Internationally Revered Speaker, Educator, and Spiritual Leader, Acclaimed Author of* Watering the Seed *and* I'll Build You a Temple – The Juhu Story

Changing our perspective and asking, "What is the lesson?" helps move us forward by getting us unstuck and immediately gaining something from each situation by entering a student's mood—regardless of the outcome.

– **CHARLES EESLEY**, *Associate Professor of Management Science and Engineering, Stanford University*

When things get overwhelming, and I feel like quitting, I've experienced great solace in taking the time to reflect on the questions given in this book. I can use these tools anytime, anywhere, and thus keep my mind in a pure, focused state.

– **TIMOTHY WOOTEN**, *Shift Lead, Wildseed Palo Alto*

My world, both internally and externally, has dramatically changed since I started listening to Vaisesika Dasa's teachings. He asks simple but essential questions that trigger deep and meaningful introspection.

– **LIJIE ZHOU**, *Site Reliability Engineer, Gusto*

Vaisesika has a way of opening your heart. He communicates with conviction and authority but lovingly manages to make even the most vulnerable topic accessible. He and his writing create a safe space to ask the hard questions.

– **MEGAN FOX, SR.**, *Program Manager, Operations Development, Construction*

Vaisesika Dasa illuminates the transformative power of "now," making each moment resonate with peace and clarity. In our rapidly advancing tech-driven world, the wisdom of these timeless questions isn't just enlightening—it's essential.
– **MAYANK AGRAWAL**, *Systems Engineer at Google and Yoga Teacher*

The topic I find most helpful is that of building good habits. Vaisesika Dasa gives practical tips for people of diverse backgrounds: youth, working professionals, householders, etc. Vaisesika Dasa's energy is contagious.
– **SWETHA RAMAIAH**, *Software Engineer, Apple*

Vaisesika Dasa's inspired self-inquiry and gentle presentation of wisdom guide the reader to perspective-altering answers about purpose, motive, life-long learning, and much more.
– **KENNEDY CARTWRIGHT**, *Community-Driven Marketing Specialist and Freelance Writer*

The most important question I've adapted from the book is, "how may I be of service?" Asking it has replaced my feelings of uselessness and depression with a sense of purpose and confidence.
– **SONALI JOG**, *Project Control Specialist, Department of Transportation*

I've always felt something was missing and knew that if I didn't adjust my mindset, nothing in this world could ever make me truly happy. *The Four Questions* has filled that void by providing me with a process by which I may experience satisfaction and growth, especially in times of difficulty.
– **ALEXANDER SEIBEL**, *Editor and Postgraduate Student*

THE FOUR QUESTIONS

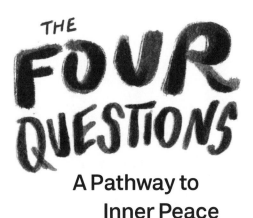

THE FOUR QUESTIONS

A Pathway to
Inner Peace

Vaiśeṣika Dāsa

THE BHAKTIVEDANTA BOOK TRUST

www.bbt.org.au
www.krishna.com

ISBN: 978-1-925850-03-1

Connect with the author:
hi@vaisesikadasa.com

For more information:
info@bbtbooks.org

Illustrations by:
Rukmini-Candrika Devi Dasi
Padma-Malini Devi Dasi
Rupa Vilasa Dasa

Book design:
Eight Eyes – eighteyes.com

TABLE OF CONTENTS

To all seekers of truth…

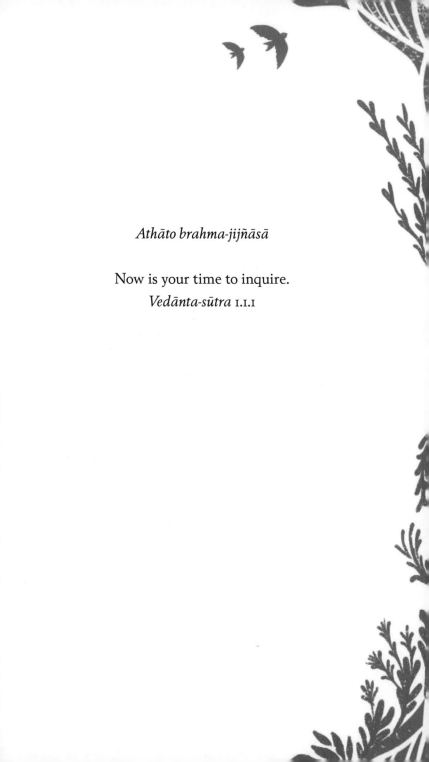

Athāto brahma-jijñāsā

Now is your time to inquire.
Vedānta-sūtra 1.1.1

Preface

Just as a deer, because of ignorance, cannot see the water within a well covered by grass, but runs after water elsewhere, the living entity covered by the material body does not see the happiness within himself, but runs after happiness in the material world.
—*Srimad-Bhagavatam* 7.13.29

Wisdom traditions throughout the world share a common thread: they remind us that we can look here, there, and everywhere for happiness outside of ourselves but that ultimately true happiness can be found only when we look within.

A musk deer spends his whole life looking for the source of the heady scent that comes from himself. He looks in caves, on the tops of hills, and along waterways, all the while unaware that the scent is coming from his own navel. We human beings are similarly absorbed: we seek pleasure externally, unaware that the source of our happiness is within ourselves. We are not material beings; we are non-material sentient parts of our source, Krishna.

Krishna, the Sanskrit name for the Supreme, means "all-attractive." All energies come from Krishna, the happiness we seek is available in Krishna, and every living being has a relationship with Krishna. Because Krishna is fully blissful and we are part of him, we are also naturally blissful. We needn't look far to find happiness; we are happy by constitution.

Most yoga classes today emphasize physical postures and breathing. These are but two small preliminary aspects of an ancient yoga practice called *ashtanga*, the eightfold path. According to the source wisdom, yoga is a complete system, seen as a ladder that one ascends, purifying one's consciousness in the step-by-step process of awakening one's original, pure consciousness, which is eternal, full of knowledge, and blissful.

The word yoga means "to connect, or link." But to connect to whom or what? Both the *Bhagavad-gita* and the *Yoga-sutras* say that the goal is to connect to our original Divine Source, who is the "soul of our soul" and the root cause of everything.

Bhakti yoga, devotional service—the path of dedicating one's senses, engaging one's tongue, ears, eyes, arms, and legs in service to the Supreme—is the top rung of the yoga ladder. The ascending rungs begin with karma yoga (the yoga of work), then jnana yoga (the yoga of intellectualizing), dhyana yoga (meditation), and finally bhakti yoga.

Patanjali Muni says in his *Yoga-sutras* 1.23: "[All] previously mentioned states of higher consciousness are attainable from devotion to Isvara [the Supreme]." And as Krishna says in the *Bhagavad-gita* (6.47), "The best yogi is the one who serves me in loving devotion." The goal of yoga is called the *sadhya*, the practice is called *sadhana*, and the practitioner is called a *sadhu*. The word sadhu comes from the term "*sadh*" which means to accomplish, attain, or succeed. A sadhu, therefore, exemplifies a spiritual practice. Sadhus are known for their wisdom, self-control, and spiritual accomplishments. They are tolerant, generous, and treat all living beings with respect.

Bhakti yoga, the process by which we naturally link to the Supreme and realize our blissful nature, begins when we ask ourselves the right questions.

Acknowledgements

My thanks to Dana Kriya Dasa, who helped mightily on the first draft of this book; to Kalachandji Dasa, Ekachakra Prana Dasa, and Anupama Dasa, the book's polish editors; to Adam Elenbaas, and Kaishori Dasi who gave invaluable feedback; to the artists, without whose expertise and creative contributions this book would not have been the same; to my friend Bhagavata Asraya with his expansive vision, and everyone on the production team.

My deepest gratitude goes to my primary spiritual teacher, my guru, Srila A. C. Bhaktivedanta Swami Prabhupada, who introduced me to the practice of asking the right questions. Students add *Srila* to the names of their teachers to indicate that their teachers not only live in the beauty of reality but also awaken it in others. *A. C.* stands for Abhay Charanaravinda, "one who is fearless." *Bhaktivedanta* is a title given to one who has acquired complete knowledge of the *Vedas*. And the honorific title *Prabhupada* means that he is a sadhu's sadhu, because he not only practiced bhakti yoga, but also taught by example, bringing thousands of new sadhus into the practice who could also teach the *Vedas* for the benefit of all living beings. Prabhupada spread Vedic wisdom to every continent of the world and showed by example how to apply it. I was a recipient of his teachings in my youth, and I continue to benefit as I enter the youth of my old age.

In 1965, at the age of seventy, Srila Prabhupada ventured out of India for the first time to bring Vedic wisdom to the West. Before arriving in America, he wrote the following in his preface to *Srimad-Bhagavatam:*

> Human society, at the present moment, is not in the darkness of oblivion. It has made rapid progress in the field of material comforts, education, and economic development throughout the entire world. But there is a pinprick somewhere in the social body at large, and therefore there are large-scale quarrels, even over less important issues. There is need of a clue as to how humanity can become one in peace, friendship, and prosperity with a common cause. *Srimad-Bhagavatam* will fill this need, for it is a cultural presentation for the respiritualization of the entire human society.

To teach the practices recommended by the *Vedas* in today's world, Prabhupada brought with him books of Vedic wisdom that he had begun to translate from the original Sanskrit. He taught what Krishna teaches in the *Gita*: that we are metaphysical beings living in physical bodies and that true knowledge means knowing the difference between spirit and matter. (7.2) Before his departure from this world in 1977, he wrote 80 books, opened 108 spiritual centers around the world, and initiated 5,000 students into the practice of bhakti yoga—all in just twelve years.

The knowledge and practices in this book, imparted to me by Srila Prabhupada, come from a bygone culture in which people lived in harmony with the gross and subtle laws of nature, kept themselves fit in body, mind, and spirit, and worked tirelessly to do good for others.

Introduction:

Questions are the Answer

The Most Powerful Punctuation Mark

Punctuation marks do practical work: a period stops us; a colon announces upcoming information; a comma divides data. But the most powerful punctuation is the question mark. It's shaped like a hook, and with it you can catch people's attention. You can snag ideas from the depths of your subconscious. It can take you beyond the mundane to the metaphysical. With a question you can discover truths of ancient wisdom, investigate your own heart, and discover your true eternal nature as an individual conscious being.

Questions Help Us Find Our Way

In his article "Self-Actual Engineer," Professor Thomas P. Seage of Arizona State University writes, "Too often, we underestimate the importance of understanding our question. When you get lost in your search for knowledge, ask yourself, 'What question was I trying to answer?' and see if that helps you find your way again." Playwright Eugene Ionesco ventures, "It is not the answer that enlightens, but the question."

Rhetoricians say that whoever is asking the questions in a conversation is leading that conversation. "Whoever has the questions, holds the power," Elisa Heikura writes in her blog, *Developerhood*. "The conversation is being directed through questions, and the person who expresses them is actually the one who decides what the conversation is about."

The *Harvard Business Review* offers this advice:

> The wellspring of all questions is wonder and curiosity and a capacity for delight. We pose and respond to queries in the belief that the magic of a conversation will produce a whole that is greater than the sum of its parts. Sustained personal engagement and motivation—in our lives as well as our work—require that we are always mindful of the transformative joy of asking and answering questions.

The question-answer format is the basis of one of the core educational processes in the West: the Socratic Method, in which "the classroom experience is a shared dialogue between teacher and students in which both are responsible for pushing the dialogue forward through questioning. The 'teacher,' or leader of the dialogue, asks probing questions to expose the values and beliefs which frame and support the thoughts and statements of the participants in the inquiry. The students ask questions as well, both of the teacher and each other."[*]

---

[*] *Speaking of Teaching*. The Center for Teaching and Learning, Stanford University, 2003.

Srimad-Bhagavatam (1.1.9) tells of an incident in which a renowned teacher, Suta, appreciates the questions of his audience, a group of sages who have gathered to ask him about the purpose of life. The sages ask, "Please, therefore, being blessed with many years, explain to us, in an easily understandable way, what you have ascertained to be the absolute and ultimate good for the people in general."

Suta replies, "O sages, I have been justly questioned by you. Your questions are worthy because they relate to Krishna and so are of relevance to the world's welfare. Only questions of this sort are capable of completely satisfying the self." (1.2.5)

I use the seemingly contradictory phrase "questions are the answer" to draw attention to the sheer magic of a question. The principle is simple and is thus one of the most overlooked miracles of the world: When you ask the right questions with the right attitude

> When you ask the right questions with the right attitude you can learn the answers to all of life's secrets.

you can learn the answers to all of life's secrets. When we sincerely ask relevant questions to qualified people, we can be sure that we'll get the answers we seek. Even before we know whom to ask, by merely formulating our questions, we have begun the process.

Those who think they already have all the answers cannot sincerely inquire and therefore will not receive solutions that will help them to progress. A colleague of mine likes to say, "There are four little words that block one's ability to learn: 'I already know that.'" But to those who are both willing to ask questions and are open-minded enough to hear the answers, the truth behind the world's mysteries is at hand.

Start Your Spiritual Quest
by Asking Questions

The word *question* comes from *quest*—to search for something—dating back to the medieval sense of romantic adventure, especially undertaken by a knight in search of the Holy Grail. And *query*—from the Latin *quaere*, "to ask"—is combined with *ad* for emphasis to form *acquire*. So, the knowledge we acquire comes from our queries, our questions.

When you ask a question, you embark on a journey. The Buddha started his journey with a question. One day he left his father's protective care and ventured outside the royal palace. There he saw sick people, old people, and people in fear and anxiety. He asked, "What is the cause of this misery?" Now *that's* a big question. And it was the bridge over which he crossed from worldly life to a life of contemplation and enlightenment.

The most important journey in your life begins when you dare to ask big questions. "But I'm no Buddha," you might protest. "How can I be compared to him?" All of us are but one question away from embarking on the path to enlightenment. It doesn't require formal education; you are born fully equipped to penetrate the mysteries of the universe. But you must inquire.

Ask Big

The opening statement of the *Vedanta-sutras* is *athato brahma jijnasa*: "Now that you're a human, inquire about the ultimate truth." Ask, "What is the purpose of life?"

Animals also ask questions. But mostly they just need to know how to survive: how to eat, sleep, mate, and defend. The yoga texts say that humans also need to ask survival questions, but to be happy, they must also ask bigger ones.

Social scientist Abraham Maslow conceived of a *hierarchy of needs* in which he points out that to be happy, humans must strive to fulfill needs—self-actualization, for example—that are above our needs for survival and comforts. In the *Bhagavad-gita*, Krishna says that a "happy human" is one who learns to control anger and lust. *Srimad-Bhagavatam* 1.2.10 states, "Be healthy. Be balanced. But do so in a way that you can vigorously inquire about the purpose of your life." In short, "Eat to live; don't live to eat."

The statement *athato brahma jijnasa* says to all humans, "Now is your chance to ask the big, important questions, ones that go beyond the survival or comfort of your body." These questions can also remind us that these physical bodies in which we reside are temporary.

"Why work just to eat?" the *Vedas* ask. "With just enough work, we can obtain our physical necessities." Due to artificial standards of living and political strife, humans can easily forget or be deprived of foodstuffs that are abundantly available from the earth. The squirrels in my backyard here in California certainly work to get their necessities, but their needs are met plentifully in every season. In winter they get a free new coat and persimmons to eat. In spring and summer, they choose among various fruits and nuts. In autumn they reap the harvest and stash nuts for the oncoming winter.

What about spiders? They literally hang out in webs, which they know how to build without instruction, and their food, bugs, are plentifully available. In undisturbed habitats, elephants find the tons of foliage they need to fill their bellies each day. *Srimad-Bhagavatam* prompts us, "Use your human energy to pursue self-realization."

The yoga texts advise, "Become a master asker." Ask penetrating, spiritual questions: "Where do I come from? What is the ultimate purpose of life? Where am I going after death?" The *Bhagavatam* tells us that as humans our prime duty is to ask questions which lead us to spiritual discovery.

The Four Questions will lead you to the solutions to life's fundamental problems and take you by the hand onto the path of the enlightened beings.

The Metaphysical Question: Why?

Armed with the questions Who? What? When? and Where? we explore and navigate the world. Then there is the standout metaphysical question, "Why?" which can take us beyond the world of matter. "Why?" questions take us into the realm of purpose, motive, and free will, which are beyond the elements and mechanics of the physical world.

Some people doubt the need for asking "Why?" because they feel that we should accept as reality only those things that we can perceive with our five material senses. Therefore, they say, the search for our spiritual selves or our relationship with the Supreme is futile. For example, the late particle physicist Victor Stenger in his 2007 book *God: The Failed Hypothesis*, subtitled *How Science Shows That God Does Not Exist*, dismisses the idea of a cosmic purpose or the need for a supreme entity. Stenger and other atheists warn that belief in a transcendent reality is blind faith because such a reality is not perceivable by our present senses.

Nonetheless, humans have always asked "Why?" We naturally hanker to understand the purpose of our lives. Is it not, then, reasonable to question where this natural human yearning comes from? When we feel thirsty, we naturally search for water. An urge indicates that an element to fulfill that urge must exist, because one cannot exist without the other. The wisdom literatures say that our natural urge for meaning, for understanding the purpose of life, similarly indicates that a metaphysical dimension must exist. Such exploration is therefore not futile but reasonable.

"Doubt is one of the important functions of the intelligence," writes Srila Prabhupada. "Blind acceptance of something does not give evidence of intelligence." (*Srimad-Bhagavatam* 3.26.30, purport) Doubt, then, is meant to bring us to a single-pointed focus on what is most valuable in life.

Blind Doubt

The bumper sticker "Question Authority" also warns about blind faith and suggests that we not accept authority until we examine it. The evil twin of blind faith, however, is blind doubt. Those who blindly doubt are also faulty: they rule out things that seem unlikely, because the subject is beyond their perceptual horizon. A boy looks at the horizon and declares it to be the world's edge. The boy's father explains that beyond the horizon are other continents not perceivable by the naked eye, but the boy doubles down on his opinion.

The yoga teachings urge us not to double down on our doubts after we receive plausible explanations. As the bumper sticker "Question Authority" also suggests when viewed from a different angle, we *should* question authority—but with the intention to learn. That is, we should ask questions of those qualified to provide us with reliable answers.

As Srila Prabhupada writes, "Doubting is not very favorable when information is received from the proper source." (*Srimad-Bhagavatam* 3.26.30, purport) In the *Bhagavad-gita*, Krishna also says that doubting the words of a well-vetted authority is nonproductive.

Those who overcome both blind faith and blind doubt are then able to open-heartedly hear reasonable explanations about the secrets that lie beyond the purview of our limited senses.

The Infinite Can Reveal Itself to Us

Why should we remain open-minded? Logically, that which is infinite has the power to reveal itself to the finite. If you say that it cannot, then you've limited the infinite, which is contradictory. Although it is not possible to understand the infinite by finite means (empirical science), if the infinite wills to reveal itself to the finite, then it can be understood.

In the words of Srila Prabhupada, "All forms of incompleteness are experienced due to incomplete knowledge of the Complete Whole."* And the Complete Whole can give complete knowledge to its parts (us) because it has that power.

By asking the right questions in the right mood, a finite being rightfully appeals to the infinite to reveal itself. This universal, non-sectarian spiritual process is found, for instance, in the New Testament:

> Ask and it will be given to you; seek and you will find; knock and the door will be opened to you. For everyone who asks receives; the one who seeks finds; and to the one who knocks, the door will be opened. (Matthew 7:7–8)

The (Un)examined Life

As stated by the Greek philosopher Socrates, "The unexamined life is not worth living." Conversely, we can also say that the examined life is inestimably valuable, because it has the potential to connect us to the metaphysical realm, that which is beyond the limitations and frailties of this material universe. According to the yoga wisdom texts, reaching the metaphysical realm is the purpose of human life, and our questions begin our journey to that realm. Just as Socrates led his students to wisdom by inducing them to ask questions, we can similarly tread the path to enlightenment by asking.

> The unexamined life is not worth living. —Socrates

---

* *Sri Isopanishad* invocation commentary.

The Quality of Your Questions Determines the Quality of Your Life

In the quest toward self-realization, the quality of your questions is vital. As author Edward Hodnett puts it, "If you do not ask the right questions, you do not get the right answers." If you ask trivial questions, you'll get trivial answers. By deliberately asking meaningful questions with precision, you can expand your consciousness and enhance the quality of your life.

In *Srimad-Bhagavatam* the teacher Sukadeva appreciates his student's question: What should he do to prepare for death? "My dear king," Sukadeva answers, "your question is glorious because it is very beneficial to all kinds of people. The answer to this question is the prime subject matter for hearing, and it is approved by all transcendentalists."

Some corporations inspire their team members to ask questions in order to probe deeper and improve their operations. *Fast Company*, a magazine that tracks successful businesses, reports: "Google's culture encourages asking questions and sharing information. Their goal is to have happier employees and they have found that when employees are allowed to ask questions, they get clarity, which leads to greater efficiency and quality in their work."[*]

Questions have more than once changed the course of history. Sir Isaac Newton's question about why apples fall from trees led to his description of gravity. "If the apple falls," he asked, "does the moon also fall?" This simple question led to Newton describing gravity and to breakthroughs in the laws of classical mechanics, which set off

---

[*] https://www.fastcompany.com/90230655/how-google-motivates-its-employees

a chain reaction in science and led to the Industrial Revolution. Albert Einstein's question "What would happen if I rode a beam of light?" led to his theory of relativity, which changed the way we view space and time.

Ask an important question—expand your world. You are lifted to the level of your questions. The quality of your questions determines the quality of your life. Live life to generate deep questions.

Albert Einstein advised, "The important thing is to not stop questioning."

The Search for Happiness

Imagine America in 1945. World War II is over. Medical researchers announce a class of "wonder drugs" that promise to eradicate most, if not all, diseases. Electronic engineers are on the verge of completing an "electronic brain"—a precursor to the modern computer—which can do five thousand computations per second. The military churns out new state-of-the-art weaponry: long-range bombers, radar, and nuclear weapons which make America and its allies appear invincible.

Today, almost eighty years later, the refinement of technology continues. With a smartphone, one can manage a small business, order products to be delivered overnight, listen to music, and watch movies chosen from catalogs containing millions of titles.

These wonders have not, however, relieved our anxieties; they've merely added new ones. We now worry about the pernicious effects of TV, streaming videos, social media, and video games. Plastics choke our oceans and waterways. Diseases appear and then mutate to circumvent our medicines. What's more, we feel entitled to miraculous technological

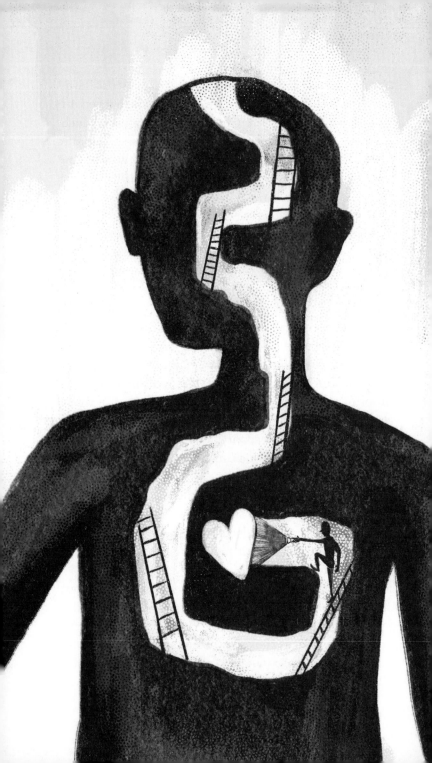

inventions and become impatient with laptop computers or smartphones if they are not noticeably faster than the previous models.

Please don't think that I'm against progress in the technological sciences. I'm not. I marvel when I hear of successful liver transplants, hip replacements, and heart surgeries. I use a smartphone, airplanes, and cars. But have our scientific discoveries and mind-blowing technologies brought us the happiness for which we had hoped? Examine any famous street in Paris, Cairo, London, or New York, and you'll find plenty of shops where you can buy clothes or coffee, have your hair styled or nails polished. But where are the shops selling the secrets to full satisfaction and a truly happy life?

The Yoga Wisdom Literatures

The wisdom texts of the Vedic tradition specialize in happiness. *Veda* means "knowledge," and the *Vedas* are ancient but ageless texts containing knowledge that lead us to happiness. We learn from them that human life is meant for self-inquiry and that whatever we do should lead to self-discovery and the purification of our body, mind, and consciousness. Vedic teachers show by example how to live a more peaceful and balanced life. They don't neglect science or technology, but instead teach us how to use them purposefully so that we can attain our full potential.

The *Vedas* include the oldest books in the world. The *Rig Veda* was written five thousand years ago. An abundance of these ancient texts, including the *Upanishads*, the *Bhagavad-gita*, and *Srimad-Bhagavatam*, give practical instruction, through philosophy and recorded history, on how to improve our lives by living in harmony with nature's laws and by rising above *samsara*, the cycle of birth and death.

Through these wisdom literatures, Vedic culture gave us Sanskrit, humankind's most perfectly constructed language, from which all other languages have evolved; *Ayurveda*, the science of medicine that not only heals but also prolongs one's life by balancing the natural forces within one's body; and meditation, the practice of which brings us multiple physical and mental benefits. Vedic culture has contributed all this to human society—and so much more.

A Culture of Inquiry

The *Vedas* reveal their wisdom through questions and answers. A student inquires, and a teacher responds—a mode of discourse we find in both the *Bhagavad-gita* and *Srimad-Bhagavatam*. In the seven hundred verses of the *Gita*, the hero of the story, Arjuna, asks questions of his teacher, or guru, Krishna. In the *Bhagavatam*, which begins from where the *Bhagavad-gita* leaves off, King Pariksit's inquiries from his guide, Sukadeva Goswami, expand into eighteen thousand verses of spiritual instruction.

Sit Near to Learn

A section of the *Vedas* called the *Upanishads* directs us to realize our spiritual nature. The word *upanishad* means "to sit near." The name implies that to learn spiritual science, one must sit close to those who have such wisdom, ask them questions, and listen attentively to their answers. The *Vedanta-sutras* embody the essential meaning of the *Upanishads*. *Vedanta* means "the conclusion of knowledge," and *sutra* means "thread." The *Vedanta-sutras* invite us to weave these threads of wisdom into the fabric of our lives.

These books present universal wisdom, speaking to us as souls rather than to our present identities related to our temporary material bodies. They advocate that we live to discover truth: reality distinguished from illusion. This wisdom and practice is accessible to any sincere seeker. Sadhus gather this wisdom, practice it, and teach it to others. They penetrate the superficial and live in the beauty of reality by asking four questions: What is my purpose? How may I be of service? What is the lesson? Where am I investing my attention right now? Anyone can become a sadhu by asking The Four Questions as they move through life.

Become a Sadhu

Dating back to prehistory, the *Vedas* have been passed down through a lineage of sadhus by the principle of "each one, teach one." Each sadhu presents the same ancient Vedic principles but makes them relevant and practical for their modern-day students. Sadhus also show us by example how to spiritualize whatever we have by using it in service to our source. The sadhu's credo is "Water the root, and all the leaves and branches are automatically nourished." The root is our source, Krishna, to whom sadhus dedicate themselves in service.

Anyone can become a sadhu by following the simplified process chalked out by sadhus

Sadhus teach us to look beyond our conceptions of material reality and investigate the subtle laws of the universe. They know that life is a classroom, that our present life is a preparation for our ultimate destination, that we are spiritual beings in material bodies, and that every living entity—indeed, all energies—come from a common, divine source that is personal and benevolent.

Above our instinct to survive is our need to feel whole. Can we find contentment even as we struggle to survive? Can we take from the world in such a way that we don't transgress the natural rights of other living beings? Can we reach our highest potential amidst a world of distractions? To all these questions and more, the sadhus say, "Yes." They also say that our feelings of incompleteness come from not having complete knowledge of our source and that an ideal way of life will uncover our virtuous qualities. Sadhus not only teach us universal spiritual practices that evoke our virtuous qualities, but also show us how to pass those practices on for the benefit of others.

A Tale of Two Sadhus

Anyone can become a sadhu by following the simplified process chalked out by sadhus. Two famous sadhus, who taught by example and left a wealth of literature, started as apparently worldly men. Dabhir and Sakar lived in fifteenth-century Bengal, India. Both were highly educated, wealthy, and influential. Both spoke several languages. Sakar was Bengal's chief minister, Dabhir its minister of finance.

Although both Dabhir and Sakar were dutiful, well loved, and materially opulent, neither was satisfied. They yearned to know the ultimate goal of life. Then they heard of a traveling monk named Chaitanya, who happened to be

camped nearby, in Ramakeli, West Bengal. Chaitanya was effulgent and charismatic, vastly learned, and yet renowned for his humility and lack of worldly attachments. Wherever he traveled, he inspired the public to chant and dance with him in spiritual rapture.

Chaitanya's daily festivals attracted tens of thousands of people. Amazed by his unparalleled influence, Dabhir and Sakar desired to meet him. They wrote him a letter requesting an audience, but after not receiving a reply for some days, they decided to go to his nearby encampment. One evening, disguised as commoners, they slipped away from their stately homes, went to the festival, and there saw Chaitanya in all his splendor. Presenting themselves as students, they asked for his tutelage, and Chaitanya welcomed the two brothers as old friends and at once accepted them as his disciples, anointing them with the spiritual names Sanatana Goswami (for Sakar) and Rupa Goswami (for Dabhir).

In time, Rupa and Sanatana returned to their posts. But both were eager to retire, join Chaitanya, and embrace a life of spiritual dedication. Rupa was first: after retiring from his government post and tying up his material affairs, he left his home and met Chaitanya at Prayag, a pilgrimage town on the bank of the Ganges. There, he presented himself to Chaitanya as a humble student and made inquiries. For the following ten days Chaitanya instructed him in the principles of bhakti yoga, devotional service to Krishna.

Sanatana had more difficulty than Rupa in breaking away from his responsibilities. When his employer, Nawab Hussain Shah, the king of Bengal, found out that Sanatana, like his brother, intended to leave his duties to join Chaitanya, he imprisoned Sanatana and told him, "Either do your duty or stay in jail." But Rupa had left Sanatana a stock of gold coins, just in case of such an emergency, and Sanatana used them to bribe the jailkeeper. In this way he escaped and made a long, clandestine trek to Varanasi, where he met Chaitanya and stayed with him to learn the science of devotional service.

Rupa Goswami and Sanatana Goswami set the standard for all those who wish to advance in spiritual life. The path opens when one asks relevant questions of a qualified teacher. No matter who we are or how learned we may be, our journey begins in earnest by asking questions in the mood of a novice. By asking the right questions in the right mood, one receives clarity and direction along their spiritual path.

From sadhus we can get answers that help us achieve our full potential. The *Bhagavad-gita* recommends, "Approach the wise in a humble mood. Serve them, and then ask them how to perfect your life." How many opportunities do we get to ask such questions during our short, busy lives? Not many. After meeting Chaitanya, therefore, Rupa wrote that the only price for entering the spiritual path is one's eagerness. "If the opportunity is available to you," he stated, "don't hesitate. Run immediately to embrace it."

In his introduction to *Bhagavad-gita As It Is* Srila Prabhupada addresses the same point:

Out of so many human beings who are suffering, there are a few who are actually inquiring about their position, as to what they are, why they are put into this awkward position and so on. Unless one is awakened to this position of questioning his suffering, unless he realizes that he doesn't want suffering but rather wants to make a solution to all suffering, then one is not to be considered a perfect human being. Humanity begins when this sort of inquiry is awakened in one's mind.

Rupa Goswami and Sanatana Goswami became Chaitanya's foremost disciples, as they were not only learned but also the most eager to inquire from him. After inquiring and then learning from him, they became world-renowned teachers and authors themselves—sadhus—writing dozens of books on the science of bhakti yoga and establishing spiritual centers that have served as places of learning for spiritual seekers from the sixteenth century up through today.

THE *Four* Questions

The Four Questions can transform your life and awaken your highest potential. Asking them of yourself regularly, and whenever you need them, will elevate your perspective and awaken your spiritual vision. This is what the Bhagavad-gita (13.22) refers to as the "vision of eternity."

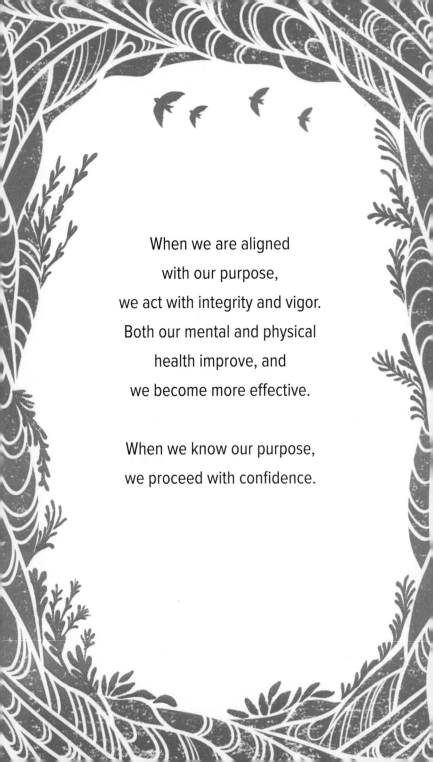

When we are aligned
with our purpose,
we act with integrity and vigor.
Both our mental and physical
health improve, and
we become more effective.

When we know our purpose,
we proceed with confidence.

Question One:
What is My Purpose?

Is it possible to go a whole day without considering the purpose behind what you are doing? Absolutely. Is it possible to work for weeks, months, years, or even a lifetime without inquiring about one's purpose? Sadly, yes—the fact is that most people don't inquire at all. The yoga wisdom texts say that humans not only *can* but *must* ask this question in order to be happy. This is why the *Vedanta-sutras* prompt us humans to use our special mental capacities to inquire about our ultimate purpose.

People often assume that they know the purpose for which they work, travel, and hold on to things. But often, they don't. Just because one is absorbed in work, adherent to a ritual, or attached to something doesn't mean that these endeavors are well thought out and reasonable. In his book

How to Win an Argument, New York University professor of rhetoric Michael Gilbert points out that the most common mistake people make when they argue is to forget the purpose for which they are arguing. "When suddenly you no longer know what you are arguing about," he advises, "check to see if the subject was changed." He also warns that many debaters are "subject switchers" and suggests that when we debate, we should remember the purpose for which we are debating. He writes, "It is very easy to find out what the argument is about: *ASK*." Once you're back on track, you can be effective.

Similarly, our minds can switch subjects on us. Have you ever picked up your cell phone to look at an email and ended up surfing the Internet? Whatever you're doing, when you ask yourself, "What is my purpose?" you realign yourself.

Are there things you're currently doing for which you've forgotten your purpose? Try asking yourself why you're doing them. We pick up habits and rituals from friends and family and then stick to them without remembering—or even knowing—their purpose.

The Cat in The Basket

A cleric was once training his students how to perform a wedding. During the cleric's tutorial, a frisky cat who lived on the church premises kept interrupting the proceedings by meowing and playing with the ceremonial items. To pacify the cat, the cleric asked one of his students to bring it a bowl of milk. After plying the rambunctious cat with milk, the cleric, a cat lover himself, stroked the cat until it became drowsy and fell asleep. Having accomplished his goal, he put the sleeping cat in a small basket in the corner of the room so that it might not disturb his teachings. Meanwhile, as the priest's students took notes regarding the details of the ceremony, they also wrote down the process for putting a frisky cat to sleep.

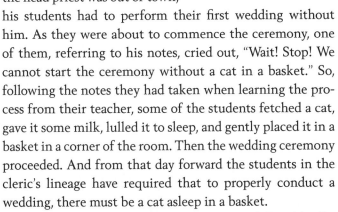

A few years later, when the head priest was out of town, his students had to perform their first wedding without him. As they were about to commence the ceremony, one of them, referring to his notes, cried out, "Wait! Stop! We cannot start the ceremony without a cat in a basket." So, following the notes they had taken when learning the process from their teacher, some of the students fetched a cat, gave it some milk, lulled it to sleep, and gently placed it in a basket in a corner of the room. Then the wedding ceremony proceeded. And from that day forward the students in the cleric's lineage have required that to properly conduct a wedding, there must be a cat asleep in a basket.

This tale points out people's tendency to follow blindly, without seeking to understand why rituals exist or why theories are accepted as truth. Are you holding on to any cat-in-the-basket rituals or presumptions in your life? If so, ask, "Are they true?" "What's their purpose?" and "What's *my* purpose?" to see if they belong.

Why Do We Exist?

Purpose is the reason for which something exists. Everything, even a tiny screw, exists for a reason. Lying on the street, the screw is insignificant. If you were to pick it up and try to sell it, you wouldn't get a penny. But when that

tiny screw is connected to the machine in which it belongs, it is of great value. The yoga texts say that living beings have a purpose for which they exist. In Sanskrit, this purpose is called dharma. The Japanese call it *ikigai*; the Chinese, *Tao*; Egyptians, *maat*. When we forget our dharma, we become miserable and unproductive.

When a wheel's axle inches out of alignment, there's friction, noise, a bumpy ride—sometimes even fire. When we similarly stray from our purpose, we develop feelings of tension, unease, and fear. Psychologists call this misalignment cognitive dissonance. For example, people who smoke are usually aware that it's bad for them, but they smoke anyway. Some people think of themselves as animal lovers but eat meat. In these cases, and many more, people feel a moral conflict between their knowledge or beliefs and their actions.

Srila Prabhupada writes, "Disturbance is due to want of an ultimate goal." (*Bhagavad-gita* 2.66, purport) When we are disturbed, we are anxious and less productive. When we are aligned with our purpose, we act with integrity and vigor. Both our mental and physical health improve, and we become more effective. When we know our purpose, we proceed with confidence.

In his novel *The Brothers Karamazov*, Fyodor Dostoyevsky writes, "The mystery of human existence lies not in just staying alive, but in finding something to live for." Working merely to stay alive is boring. Working for a cause that one is willing to die for is thrilling. Dr. Martin Luther King Jr. stated, "Life is not worth living until you have found something worth dying for."

The great philosopher Aristotle urges people to analyze the purpose for which they exist. An anonymous author summarizes Aristotle's thoughts about purpose on the blog, *The Great Conversation*:

> Aristotle argues that the ultimate purpose for humans will be something that we desire for the sake of itself and never for the sake of anything else. For example, imagine a curious adolescent who ceaselessly asks 'why' to every answer you provide him. Why are you going to school? To earn a degree. Why do you want a degree? I need a degree to obtain employment. Why do you want a job? I need a job so that I can earn money to buy the things I need, such as a house, clothes, food, etc. Why do you need all that? Those things will make me happy. Why do you want to be happy? At this point you realize that there is no further answer. You want to be happy for the sake of being happy, and not for the sake of something else.[*]

"What is my purpose?" is the most important question we humans can ask. People who are conscious of *why* they are doing what they are doing know which path to follow and thus make better choices on life's journey. As humans we

---

[*] https://orwell1627.wordpress.com/2013/06/30/aristotles-purpose-of-life/

can choose to dedicate our lives to whatever we wish. Such independence, however, carries the weight of responsibility for our choices.

Human Responsibility

In the third chapter of the *Bhagavad-gita*, Krishna explains that the essence of human responsibility is *yajna*, sacrifice—the act of giving up something valuable to someone important or worthy. Because we receive a multitude of gifts from our source, we must reciprocate in gratitude by giving something back. By giving, we grow.

For example, those who dedicate the results of their work to the Supreme, perhaps giving a portion of what they earn or volunteering for a spiritual cause, are performing *yajna*. Conversely, those who work solely for themselves take on a cosmic debt called karma, which obligates the debtor to work hard. Those who take from nature without acknowledging the source of their bounty are compared to thieves who can never be happy. Thus, giving is our duty because we are part of the Complete Whole.

The Complete Whole is known by many names: Krishna, Allah, Yahweh, the Supreme. Ultimately, all these names refer to the same Divine Source from whom everything emanates. The whole of existence is compared to a tree. By *yajna*, we water the root of this tree and thereby nourish ourselves, who are like its branches and leaves. Those who neglect the root and instead water the leaves and branches in an attempt to satisfy themselves independently actually fail to nourish themselves. Krishna therefore remarks, "My dear Arjuna, living only for the satisfaction of the senses, a person lives in vain."

Marry Your Purpose

Yoga texts describe a phenomenon called *niyamagraha*, a Sanskrit term with two meanings. The first is to be divorced from one's purpose. Have you ever practiced something or followed a rule or routine just for the sake of doing it, without knowing the purpose behind it? This is called *niyamagraha*. Asking "What's my purpose?" gives us focus and clarity, brings meaning to our actions, and helps us ignore distractions.

The second meaning of *niyamagraha* is to stop trying altogether. To advance in any discipline, one must have a systematic practice. Those who stop practicing make no advancement. In other words, one should practice regularly, but one should also be clear on the purpose of the practice. Marrying our purpose means that we have a clear idea why we exist and actively work toward realizing that purpose.

Write Down Your Priorities

To determine your purpose in life, it can help to first list and order your priorities. When the COVID-19 pandemic began in 2020, I took the time to sit in a distraction-free setting and write down my priorities. This gave me a renewed sense of purpose.

In her book *The Top Five Regrets of the Dying*, author Bronnie Ware points out that people tend to move blithely through life without considering what's important—until they get some indication that death is coming. She recommends that we not wait until the end of life to decide what is most important to us. Otherwise, as the title of her book suggests, we will be full of regrets.

Try this: Set aside some time to sit down with pen and paper and ask yourself, "What are my priorities?" At the top of the page write, "What is most important to me?" and then just start brainstorming. You don't have to worry about coming up with the perfect answers; just take the time to write down whatever comes to your mind.

Once you've come up with an initial list, mull it over, process it. Then try reading it to mentors, close friends, and trusted family members. Ask them, "What do you think?" The more you churn your priorities, thinking them over and discussing them with others, the clearer they become and the more you'll feel a fixity of purpose. In my experience, when people hear such a list, they feel inspired and want to make their own lists. When I sent a copy of my priorities to a scholarly friend, for instance, he wrote back a commentary on each one, mentioning philosophical parallels given by ancient thinkers. Other friends sent back a list of their own.

The physical process of writing is a means of taking something that is subtle—a thought or idea—and making it tangible, giving it shape. Studies demonstrate how powerful and transformative it is to write down your goals and intentions, and how this simple act can bring you into greater alignment with those goals. A 2015 study conducted by the Dominican University of California found that those who wrote down their goals were far more likely to succeed than those who either did not have goals or did not solidify them by writing them down.[*] As soon as you identify your priorities and write them down, you will immediately, almost

---

[*] https://scholar.dominican.edu/cgi/viewcontent.cgi?article=1265&context=news-releases

magically, start to conceive goals aligned with your values, which will help you identify your life's purpose.

The Magic of Asking

As soon as we sincerely ask, "What is my purpose?" we'll be provided the intelligence to answer the question. There is a divine plan for every one of us. The only reason we may not be aware of it is that we're not asking this question.

When we start asking the right questions and making them a part of our daily practice and meditation, we will become aware of a guiding inner voice. In the Bible, Elijah is reassured during a disaster by the "still, small voice" within. Prabhupada writes, "Every living being has his intelligence, and this intelligence, being the direction of some higher authority, is just like a father giving direction to his son. The higher authority, who resides within each individual living being, is the Superself." By acknowledging the Super-self, we will also see and appreciate the serendipity in the events of our lives. This is one of the ironclad principles mentioned in the *Bhagavad-gita:* Our sincerity is infallibly effective.

Stay Hungry and Humble

Sincerity creates a hunger to know the truth and to improve ourselves. Just as the hungrier we are for food, the more we can eat and digest, similarly the keener we are to know, the more open we are to receive answers and guidance from within. The saint Queen Kunti advises, therefore, that we keep ourselves in the state of spiritual hunger called *akincana. Akincana* means to feel oneself a humble beginner, devoid of entitlement and helplessly dependent on a higher power. Literally, *akincana* means "without anything." The *akincana* mind is always ready for more. Queen Kunti said, "If you think you're smart, beautiful, wealthy, or prestigious, then you are already full." Srila Prabhupada writes in a *Bhagavad-gita* purport (12.8–12), "Knowledge begins with humility."

We can begin to help ourselves as soon as we sincerely admit that we need help. When we see that we're completely helpless, we are in the perfect position to be sincere. In other words, if we are sincerely humble and ask for direction, we will be given the intelligence to unlock the answers that bring out the highest purpose of life.

Axiomatic Truth and Aligned Purpose

Problem solving in geometry starts with a premise. We can't solve a problem that says, "Given nothing, solve for x." And, as Aristotle noted, unless we base our hypotheses on axiomatic truth, our thought processes will be susceptible to infinite regress and we won't get anywhere. Of course, it's best if premises are true!

The premise, or axiom, in yoga teachings is that we are non-material entities. That is, we are categorically different from matter, a fact we can see through the incongruity and frustration we feel as we deal with matter.

I often feel this frustration. For example, I want to stay healthy and young, so I exercise every day and am careful about what I eat. But despite my efforts, the expiration dates on my body parts are approaching, as I'm beginning to notice. My problem starts with thinking that I am my body. My problem is solved when I apply the axiomatic truth of the *Vedas:* Consciousness is different from matter. We are conscious entities inhabiting temporary material bodies.

The yogic teachings explain that consciousness and inert matter are different categories of energy. If we overlook this and become infatuated with the ever-changing forms of matter, we remain unsatisfied, because the happiness we get from material interactions has a beginning and an end. The same teachings say that material happiness is a misnomer because material desire is by definition unfulfillable; trying to satisfy it is like trying to taste sweetness by licking the glass on the outside of a bottle of honey.

The wisdom literatures make a study of happiness. *Real* happiness does not come and go, but is everlasting. We taste the highest degree of happiness through *yajna*, sacrifice. We are happier when we give rather than take. We feel most satisfied when our service is selfless, motivated by love, not by greed—when we direct our attention to the substantive rather than the trivial and align ourselves with our spiritual purpose. The wisdom literatures, therefore, present us with an axiomatic truth: we are not material. We are spiritual entities, not part of the material world.

Questions by the Sages

We each have an individual purpose in life—our dharma, or duty—to utilize our unique gifts and talents in service. But we also all share an ultimate purpose.

The *Bhagavatam* (1.1.9) opens with a group of sages gathered at a tranquil forest called Naimisaranya to ask

questions about the ultimate purpose of life. The sages ask potent questions to the wisest among them, Suta Goswami.

One of the questions the sages ask is, "What is the absolute and ultimate good for everyone, without exception?" Suta Goswami's answer is that the universal dharma, the highest purpose for everyone, is to attain loving connection and service to our Original Divine Source, Krishna, who is love personified. Such service, when unselfish and uninterrupted, brings about complete self-satisfaction. (1.2.6) And how can we align ourselves with this universal dharma? By asking the next of The Four Questions!

KEY TAKEAWAYS

- Base your life on the right axiom: "You are not your material body or mind."

- The supreme purpose that we all share is "to revive our loving connection with our Original Divine Source."

- Be *akincana*—stay humble and maintain a beginner's mindset and you'll be able to receive and learn more.

- We are happier when we give rather than take.

- Material happiness is a misnomer because material desire is by definition unfulfillable.

JOURNAL PROMPTS

Set a timer for ten minutes and write down any responses that come to mind when you ask yourself, "What are my priorities?"

Then, go through your list and put the items in their order of importance to you. When you have your priorities in order, make your list visible so that you can read it daily.

(Repeat this practice periodically, or whenever you feel your priorities need to be adjusted.)

Selfless service
gives one a taste of
natural satisfaction
and happiness.

By giving, one grows.

Question Two:
How May I Be of Service?

Our second question—"How may I be of service?"—is powerful because according to the bhakti teachings, we are inherently service givers. Our fundamental nature is to contribute to a greater good. Factually, our lives are meant for service, and when we embrace that idea, we feel happy. *Srimad-Bhagavatam* (1.2.6) says that when we do "unmotivated and uninterrupted" service to our original conscious source, we feel satisfied. *Unmotivated service* means service for which we are not seeking any personal gain, not even recognition. *Uninterrupted* means that we continue our service despite obstacles. Paradoxically, serving without expecting recognition or reward is most rewarding.

Choose Your Path—Enjoyment, Renunciation, or Dedication

Which is the right path for you? Before we explore this question, let's look at some of the paths the yoga literatures tell us we can choose to follow.

The ancient texts describe three general paths: the path of material enjoyment, the path of renouncing the material world, and the path of dedication, devotional service to the Supreme. The path of material enjoyment means to try as hard as we can to get comfortable in life and enjoy the temporary creature comforts this world has to offer. People have myriad means of going about this, but all of them are ultimately futile because we are eternal spiritual beings, categorically different from matter and its temporary manifestations. Many writings—not only yoga texts, but also songs and poems—confirm this fact. The Rolling Stones sing, "I Can't Get No Satisfaction"; Shakespeare writes in *Macbeth*, "Life's but a walking shadow, a poor player, that struts and frets his hour upon the stage, and then is heard no more. It is a tale told by an idiot, full of sound and fury, signifying nothing." Thus, due to matter's inherent inability to provide lasting satisfaction, this path is not recommended.

The second path is to renounce the material world after one has realized that it is a troublesome place full of all sorts of miseries. An aspirant on the renunciate's path thinks, "I'm going to unload this whole thing, just give it up. I'll be detached from everything and everyone."

The problem with this path is that as conscious living beings we all have an inherent spirit of attachment. Our nature is to be attached to something or someone. According to a study conducted by Brett Ford of the University of California, Berkeley, published in the *Journal*

of Experimental Psychology, human happiness "is linked to social engagement and helping others." Many prisons include cells designed for solitary confinement, which is considered the most extreme form of punishment. In such a cell the captive cannot see outside or have meaningful human contact. The United Nations has deemed that holding someone in this environment for fifteen days or more is a form of torture.

The bhakti yoga teachings therefore recommend that one associate with high-minded people. This will not only fulfill our need for social interaction but will also give us an opportunity to develop noble qualities by their association. As the saying goes, "Show me your friends and I'll show you your future." The bhakti yoga teachings similarly recommend that we choose our associates with care.

Another problem with the path of detachment is that the things renunciants try to give up aren't theirs to begin with. Let's say I stroll into a Bank of America and declare that I am renouncing the bank and all the money in it. The bankers would think I'm crazy—the money in the bank isn't mine. In a broader sense, none of the temporary things of this world are ours; they are all on loan and will eventually be repossessed.

The third path, the middle path, is bhakti yoga, the path of dedication—devotional service. One who follows this path is still involved with the world, still connected with other people, still engaged in loving relationships, and is still attached, but the bhakti yogi's attachment is not material. The bhakti yogis are attached to using everything in their sphere of influence to establish a spiritual connection and engage in relationships that have a spiritual foundation. This is the proper use of our inherent love and attachment.

And that's why the bhakti path is so powerful—because we are by nature active, loving, and attached.

Bhakti yoga, the path of dedication, helps us engage with the world in an enlightened way. As we move about the world, we can remain naturally balanced by dedicating our thoughts, words and activities to the service of the Supreme Person.

Refining Our Service Propensity

If you find yourself in a frustrating situation or feel like you're caught in a whirlpool of anxiety and don't know how to get out, try asking yourself, "How may I be of service? How can I serve in this situation?" You'll find clarity of mind, for the very question connects you to your *sanatana-dharma*, your eternal nature. *Sanatana* means eternal; dharma means our purpose, duty, or nature. Just as the dharma of sugar is sweetness and the dharma of water is liquidity, the dharma of the soul, or *atma*, is to serve. Every one of us is already engaged in the service of someone or something. As Bob Dylan sang, "It may be the devil or it may be the Lord, but you're gonna have to serve somebody."*

---

* Bob Dylan, "Gotta Serve Somebody," 1979.

There are lower forms of service, but they inhibit our progressive advancement in life. Many people, for instance, are servants of their senses. They "live to eat" or are enslaved by addiction to one substance or another. Driven by the idea of attaining happiness through sensual enjoyment, our mind and senses can impel us to act in various—and often self-destructive—ways. Rupa Goswami, after meeting Chaitanya, lamented, "For how long have I obeyed the bad masters that are my senses? They were always telling me what to do, and I never questioned them. They never gave me time off, and they never gave me mercy. I will no longer obey them. Now I ask only for service to Krishna." (*Caitanya-caritamrta, Madhya-lila* 22.16, paraphrased)

Selfless Service

People have various motives for serving, one of which may be the expectation of something in return. But sincere, selfless service means that one doesn't want anything for oneself; one is satisfied simply to serve. And such service to the Supreme—done purely for the sake of the service itself without any expectation of recognition or reward—frees one from the control of the senses and promotes spiritual progress. Selfless service gives one a taste of natural satisfaction and happiness. By giving, one grows.

This principle came to life for me while I was living in a monastery. One morning, as a newly ordained monk, I was especially hungry. When the breakfast bell rang, I jumped up and ran to the dining hall with one thought in mind: "I want to eat." When I arrived, however, there was a snag. The monk whose turn it was to serve breakfast that day was absent, and it was my duty to fill in for him. I was so hungry; the last thing I wanted to do was delay my eating and serve food to others. But then I remembered my teacher's advice: to serve selflessly. So rather than give in to my stomach's demand to eat as soon as I could, I decided to try being fully present while serving the others. As soon as I began, I felt better. My hunger was replaced with a higher sense of satisfaction, which made a lasting impression on me. Serving selflessly was not just a slogan; it was the key to my happiness.

Selfless service stems from love. Such service directed toward Krishna, our Original Divine Source, is bhakti yoga. Just as watering the root of a tree nourishes all its branches, devotional service ensures the welfare of all aspects of our lives. Such a selfless perspective also properly adjusts our relationships with material resources. Those enlivened by this bhakti-infused consciousness naturally live by the principle of *yukta-vairagya*, or feasible renunciation. They engage all their material resources in loving service to the Supreme. Whereas trying to own and exploit material things for one's own pleasure breeds anxiety and disappointment, applying this principle of loving renunciation yields everlasting happiness.

The Road to Dissatisfaction

To achieve happiness by taking oneself out of the center might at first seem counterintuitive. "How can *I* be served?" one might wonder. "Why aren't more people serving *me*? My children aren't serving me well enough, my spouse isn't doing enough for me, my friends aren't doing enough for me, and the government isn't doing enough for me. Why don't they do more?" Beware: Such false expectations guarantee disappointment.

Another question that can lead one in the wrong direction is, "How can I get more comfortable in life?" Of course, we need a modicum of comfort. As Srila Prabhupada writes, "To keep themselves fit, [bhakti yogis] must therefore place themselves in a normal condition of life." (*Srimad-Bhagavatam* 8.2.30, purport) But what constitutes a "normal" condition varies from person to person. We must have what we need to be comfortable enough to go on asking good questions. But if we make comfort our priority, we are fated to live in frustration, as the material world is not designed to serve such a purpose. One cannot wrest lasting satisfaction from fleeting pleasures.

This axiomatic truth is also backed by modern science. In the 2012 documentary *Happy*, filmmaker Roko Belic chronicles psychologists' findings on happiness. His film addresses what is known as the hedonic treadmill: that whatever material gains a person achieves, he or she quickly becomes accustomed to them and wants more. The "joy" of buying a new car is short-lived because of all the anxieties that come with its maintenance. What's more, the law of diminishing returns says that buying a second new car will bring even less of that fleeting joy than one received upon buying the first one. The ancient yoga wisdom literatures point out that materialism is not limited to buying things—all activities based on sense pleasure share this temporality and subsequent inability to provide the eternal happiness for which everyone hankers.

Reversing Dissatisfaction

We can reverse our dissatisfaction by asking ourselves how we may be of service. Bhakti yoga texts explain that the best way to engage the mind is to train it to always be thinking of how to do good for others. In his popular book *How to Win Friends and Influence People*, Dale Carnegie touches on a similar point: "The world is full of people who are grabbing and self-seeking. So, the rare individual who unselfishly tries to serve others has an enormous advantage."

The service attitude gives us the advantage of removing ourselves from the center. When we serve, we relieve the pressure and frustration that results from living as though everything revolves around us. Ask yourself this question "How may I be of service?" By asking this question, we rise above the false expectations that breed disappointment. We are then reinstated in our natural happy state of consciousness.

Sanatana Goswami's Questions to Chaitanya

As Chaitanya's disciple, Sanatana Goswami asked probing questions. "People believe that I am a great learned man," he said, "and I am so foolish that I believe it myself. But what to speak of being learned, I don't even know who I am. Who am I? And why do I suffer in material life?" (*Caitanya-caritamrta, Madhya-lila* 20.100–103)

Chaitanya's answer is that our constitutional position is to engage in divine service, because we are all parts and parcels of Krishna, as sparks are part of a fire. Just as a spark separated from a fire soon loses its glow, we living beings, separated from serving Krishna, gradually lose our spiritual happiness. And just as a spark returned to the fire is reignited, we, when reconnected with our service to Krishna, revive our inherent happiness. (*Caitanya-caritamrta, Madhya-lila* 20.108–109)

See Through the Eyes of Service

I once saw a short film about a man whose morning didn't go well. Every aspect of his routine annoyed him, starting with a burned-out light bulb and an empty tube of toothpaste—nothing in the house seemed to work. When the man was backing out of his driveway, a kid on a skateboard cut him off, and the man thought, "Why does that kid *always* go behind me when I'm pulling out? Hasn't he got a brain?" At his usual coffee shop, there was a long line. "I have to wait so long," he complained to himself. "This is horrible!" Someone cut in front of him, and he thought, "Why is she so inconsiderate?" The barista seemed to take forever, and by the time the man finally got his coffee and sat down, he felt totally frustrated. At that moment, a stranger walked up to him, handed him a pair of glasses, and said, "Please try these on." The camera then pans to the label on the glasses' case—EYES OF SERVICE.

When the man put on the glasses, he could see that everyone he had encountered was grappling with some problem. He could see a digital readout on each person's chest that showed the specific problem each of them was facing. The kid who rode the skateboard behind his car was in a hyperactive state due to a lack of attention from his family. The woman had absentmindedly cut him off because she had just found out that her husband had cancer. The barista was struggling to overcome a drug addiction but was trying his best to cheerfully serve the customers.

Upon seeing the plight of each person he had met, the man felt an urge to do something to help them. His mind and heart transformed, his frustration abated, he could see that the inconveniences he had felt were trivial, and a smile came over his face. Through the glasses he now saw the people whom he had perceived as offensive to be fellow travelers facing the same kinds of struggles as he. As the impulse to help these people increased, so too did his sense of purpose, peace of mind, and happiness. As Krishna says in *Bhagavad-gita* (6.32), "He is a perfect yogi who, by comparison to his own self, sees the true equality of all beings, in both their happiness and their distress, O Arjuna!"

Fan the Spark

A service attitude changes our relationship with the world, and the more we expand that attitude, the more we feel fulfilled. This is the occupation of a spiritualist: to recognize and fan the spiritual spark in others. The happiest people are those who empathize with the sufferings of others and who try to help them. The wisdom texts say that the best way to serve others is to give them spiritual knowledge.

No More Misery

Bhaktivinoda Thakura, a famous teacher of bhakti yoga, wrote in one of his Bengali songs: "When you declare yourself a servant of the Supreme, all your misery will vanish." This one line alone can change your life. As we move about the world, expecting others to serve us, we feel exhausted. But when we ask ourselves, "How may I be of service?" we feel invigorated.

It's uncanny how one can become happier through service. As wannabe controllers, we face inevitable shortfalls. But as servants, we realize ever-increasing facility. Great thinkers consistently present service as the way to thrive:

- Saint Francis of Assisi: "For it is in giving that we receive."

- Mahatma Gandhi: "The best way to find yourself is to lose yourself in the service of others."

- Author Maya Angelou: "I have found that among its other benefits, giving liberates the soul of the giver."

- Boxing champion and human activist Muhammed Ali: "Service to others is the rent you pay for your room here on earth."

Finding Your Specific Service

Hearing these glorifications of service, you may wonder, "What is *my* service in this world?" Sometimes it takes a little practice to develop a service mood before one finds the specific ways in which one is empowered, but once you identify a service that comes naturally to you and enlivens you, it can grow into your lifetime service. If you just stay open to the idea and keep asking yourself how *you* can serve, then you'll eventually find your service niche.

Service often comes through people who already have service. In the bhakti tradition one normally receives service from a venerable sadhu. If you go to a sadhu already engaged in meaningful service and ask, "Is there something I can do to assist you?" they will be grateful and find a way for you to help. It usually starts small: you get a little service to do; then, when you put your heart into it, the service expands over time and becomes a bigger part of your life. So, if you find an experienced sadhu doing a service that inspires you and aligns with your values, take the opportunity to ask if you can help.

Nuances of Service

But won't we become everyone's doormat if we're always just trying to serve? Won't people just walk all over us? No; having a service attitude doesn't mean that we just bend to everybody's will and allow them to take advantage of us. But it does mean that we should use our intelligence to discover how we can improve any situation by being service-minded. What's more, we are not obligated to serve those who are simply out to exploit us. In this matter, discretion is the better part of valor.

Service manifests in various ways, and because life is full of diversity, there are unlimited ways to serve and countless nuances to consider when applying one's service attitude. Arjuna, for instance, served by using martial arts on a battlefield to fight against injustice and to protect the innocent. His service was to fight, as he was a warrior by nature and profession.

Of course, under most circumstances, such violence would be criminal. But the message of the *Gita* is clear: "Everything can be used in service." What's more, Krishna says in the *Gita* that even the slightest gesture made in service to the Supreme is potent. It all boils down to motive. The fulcrum of power lies in our intent.

Sometimes we may feel that our service is insignificant, that it isn't enough. "If I can't do everything," we may think, "I might as well do nothing." This tendency is addressed in a story from the *Ramayana*, the longest epic poem in history.

The hero, Rama, was building a bridge across the ocean to get to Lanka and rescue his wife, Sita, who had been kidnapped. A squirrel had been throwing little pebbles into the water to help build the bridge. To others, the squirrel didn't seem to be doing anything of value, but Rama reprimanded the squirrel's critics: "This squirrel's service is just as important as anyone else's. He is doing service according to his capacity."

What may seem insignificant may be very significant on a deeper level. As the saying goes, "It's the thought that counts." In the same *Ramayana* we hear about Jatayu, the king of birds who had grown old and weary. Despite his old age, however, he stepped up to fight the powerful Ravana, just as Ravana kidnapped Sita, Rama's wife. Jatayu was obviously no match for Ravana in physical strength. But even though Jatayu died in the fight, Rama so much appreciated his service that he personally performed Jatayu's last rights with deep affection and gratitude.

KEY TAKEAWAYS

- Selfless service means doing something favorable for someone else *without seeking credit for doing it.*

- The middle path—bhakti—allows us to live a spiritual life in the material world.

- The secret to happiness is not to renounce material resources, but to engage everything in service to the Divine.

- See through the eyes of service to empathize with others.

- We most often get meaningful service through people who already have such service.

JOURNAL PROMPTS

Fan the spark: Give encouragement or appreciation to someone. Write down how it makes you feel.

Perform an anonymous act of service for someone—no matter how small—remembering that an essential element of that service is to not seek credit for doing it.

....
....
....
....
....
....
....
....
....
....
....
....
....
....
....
....
....
....

Instead of asking,
"Why me? Why am I the victim?"
ask, "What is the lesson?"

When you engage in this practice,
you'll find that your intelligence
will be divinely empowered
to find the lessons in life's events.

Question Three:
What Is the Lesson?

The world often moves in ways contrary to our plans. We may have an idea of how things should go—we may even do everything required to make them happen—still, we meet with reversals. When things go wrong, rather than ask, "Why me?" and dig oneself into an ever-deepening hole, we can instead ask our third question: "What is the lesson?"

It may not be easy. Your mind may balk at asking this question and default to the easier role of being a victim and becoming morose. To consistently ask "What is the lesson?" requires practice, diligence, and an introspective attitude. We humans are designed to learn from experience, so it's not only possible, but natural. What's more, the search for lessons brings meaning to life. We come to see how so-called reversals of fortune, even calamities, can be blessings in disguise. By asking this third question and looking for the lesson, you can rewrite your mind's tendency to take false shelter of victimhood and instead transform the experience into an opportunity for learning.

Your Attitude Determines Your Altitude

Austrian neurologist, psychologist, philosopher, and author Victor Frankl, who was imprisoned in concentration camps and whose wife and family were killed by the Nazis, wrote, "Everything can be taken from a man but one thing: the last of human freedoms—to choose one's attitude in any given set of circumstances, to choose one's own way." What an uplifting approach to life!

I knew someone who had a similar approach. Bhakti Tirtha Swami was a vibrant and charismatic monk, teacher and leader who spent decades traveling the world and touching countless lives with his words and example. In 2004 he was diagnosed with an acute form of melanoma cancer, and despite all efforts, his condition soon worsened. In his final days, his body was ravaged: he had a broken collar bone, pervasive tumors, and his leg had to be amputated. He was so weak that he couldn't even turn over in his bed without help. But despite these dire conditions, he sought the lessons to be learned from this experience and grew. Sharing profound realizations from his bed, he gave inspirational classes to thousands. And at the peak of his illness, just before passing away, he spoke this prayer:

I can understand, Dear Lord, that you have blessed me so much by giving me some tangible experience of illness and helping me transcend my bodily consciousness. Because I am now submerged in bodily suffering, I can better perceive the unlimited tricks of my false ego. I can even understand the nature of my stagnations much better. I beg you Dear Lord, even if it means increasing my bodily discomfort, please do whatever is necessary to help me become a better servant of You and Your servants.*

Bhakti Tirtha Swami left his body in 2005, but even in his excruciatingly painful physical condition, in his final moments he remained in a state of bliss. Because of his impeccable attitude, he not only rose above his bodily pains, but was also able to take—and give—lessons from his experience.

Attitude is defined as "A settled way of thinking or feeling about someone or something; typically, one that is reflected in a person's behavior." In short, our attitude leads to our behavior. People who learn to adjust their attitudes rise above whatever obstacles might seem to be in their way and often surpass whatever goals they had imagined.

Baseball pitcher Jim Abbott was born with only one hand. As a boy, he was rejected by coaches who didn't think he could play. When he complained to his father, however, his father replied that the reason why he wasn't accepted by coaches wasn't because of his physique; it was because he wasn't good enough at baseball. In response, Abbott figured out how to maneuver his glove so that he could both pitch and field the ball, and he practiced until he got good enough to make a team. In college he was named the nation's best

---

* https://www.facebook.com/HHBTS108/
   photos/a.539674099546897/1133875300126771

amateur athlete, as a major league professional he threw a no-hitter for the New York Yankees, and went on to have a successful career as a motivational speaker.

The World is a Classroom

Classrooms are places dedicated to learning. Students listen and engage in discussion to learn a skill or subject. After leaving the classroom, they put their knowledge to practical use. We can be perpetual students, as life is our teacher. Every circumstance is an opportunity to learn. When we ask, "What is the lesson?" the universe becomes our schoolhouse. Whoever passes the tests reaches their highest potential even, or especially, in adversity. And upon graduation we can reach our ultimate destination: unbounded happiness due to our being situated in pure, spiritual consciousness.

We hear from the sage Sukadeva that the purpose of human life is to learn how to remember the Supreme at the time of death, which can come at any moment. He recommends that we use every situation we encounter to practice. We should be so practiced in remembering the Supreme that we naturally do it all the time, regardless of whether things go "right" or "wrong."

Our present life is not our ultimate destination; it's a stopover. While here, we're meant to develop impeccable qualities. The *Bhagavad-gita* (16.1-3) lists some of them:

Fearlessness; purification of one's existence; cultivation of spiritual knowledge; charity; self-control; performance of sacrifice; search for wisdom; simplicity; nonviolence; truthfulness; freedom from anger; tranquility; aversion to faultfinding; compassion for all living entities; freedom from covetousness;

gentleness; modesty; steady determination; vigor; forgiveness; fortitude; cleanliness; and freedom from envy and from the passion for honor.

These transcendental qualities, Krishna tells Arjuna, are indications of a divine nature. When we look for the lessons in both our struggles and victories, we awaken these qualities, which are eternally present within us. These divine qualities are prerequisites for an intimate relationship with the Supreme and, resultantly, eternal happiness.

Srimad-Bhagavatam (11.7.20) teaches that by taking the world as a classroom, we develop the intelligence to learn lessons from all our interactions: "An intelligent person, expert in perceiving the world around him and in applying sound logic, can achieve real benefit through his own intelligence. Thus sometimes one acts as one's own instructing spiritual master."

The Classroom of Relationships

There are several different classrooms in the cosmic schoolhouse. In the classroom of relationships, we learn that "Your mate is your mirror." That is, those closest to us often give us feedback that no one else is willing to give. People have difficulty cooperating because each of us has

a unique way of seeing the world. To succeed while living and working with others, then, we must be able to tolerate differences of ideas and ways of doing things until we find a way to harmonize them. Then, cooperation is possible. Therefore, for the sake of cooperation, it's best to avoid ultimatums. The mind tends to say, "If I can't have it my way, I quit." But to consider others' preferences alongside one's own is an enlightened state that yields progress.

Relationships thrive or fail based on the attention we give them. Give someone your full attention and see what happens. They are likely to notice, since most people at best give only divided attention to others. Spoiled persons think of only their own needs, make ultimatums, and are stingy about giving others attention. A student in the classroom of relationships learns the invaluable lesson that giving goes a long way and also feels better than receiving. Didn't our mothers teach us that it is better to give than to receive?

The Classroom of Sacrifice

In the classroom of sacrifice students learn that they are dependent on higher forces to survive, let alone fulfill their desires. To think that one deserves something for nothing is delusional. We pay a price for everything, and nothing good comes without sacrifice. Krishna confirms this in the *Gita* (4.31): "Without sacrifice one can never live happily in this life or on this planet: what then of the next?" To make progress one must learn to sacrifice.

The word *sacrifice* derives from the Latin *sacrificum*, which means "the act of giving up one thing for another." *Sacrifice* also means "to make sacred." The lesson we learn in the classroom of sacrifice is that by giving, we grow. And when we give to the Supreme, our lives become sacred.

The Classroom of Service

Toddlers are by nature self-centered and think only of their own needs. But as they grow and develop, they learn the value of sharing. In "The Way Children Are," the Center for Parenting Education describes how children develop empathy gradually, over time:

> While it may be frustrating to have children who appear to be self-centered, unrelenting, and impulsive, it can be comforting to learn that these traits are typical of the development of all children. It is only over time that children gradually learn:
>
> - that they are not the center of the universe and that other people exist who have feelings and needs that are not necessarily the same as their own;
>
> - that they can and sometimes have to wait before getting or doing what they want;
>
> - that they can gain improved judgment as a result of life experiences.*

"Oh look—she shared a toy!" a parent might react, seeing their child maturing. "She's growing up!" Adolescents often volunteer for a cause they believe in—another sign that they are thinking of the needs of others. First they share with family, then with people of their town, then with others around the world, then they may consider, "What is the best thing I can do for people everywhere?" And finally, they

---

* https://centerforparentingeducation.org/library-of-articles/child-development/way-children/

may realize how by serving the Supreme, all living entities within the universe are served.

In the teachings of bhakti, the definition of successful human life is that one develops the mindset to do good for all living entities. That mindset is developed in the classroom of service.

The Classroom of Tolerance

In the *Gita*, Krishna emphasizes the importance of tolerance, and Chaitanya teaches, "one should be more tolerant than the tree," which endures the weather and seasons. One must tolerate inconveniences and other people's minor offences. Have you ever been insulted, over-reacted, and then wished you hadn't? Before email, people wrote letters on paper and mailed them. I once wrote a letter of complaint to a friend who had given me something, and then, later, taken it back. He claimed that it had been a loan, but I remembered that it was a gift. Luckily, before I mailed the letter, I read it to a mutual friend, and they advised me: "Don't send that letter. It's not worth degrading your relationship." I thought about it and then threw the letter in the recycling bin. Had it been an email instead of a letter, I might have clicked on the send button and ruined a longtime friendship.

A moment of intolerance can ruin one's life; a moment of tolerance can change our perspective on life. My friend Vraj, who does conflict resolution for a living, taught me that there is an inverse relationship between emotion and rational thought. When you're angry, you don't think clearly. The angrier, sadder, or more attached you are, the more your power of discretion decreases.

When my wife and I first moved to the Bay Area, there was an incident of road rage near our home. A man on a motorcycle got into a dispute with a man driving a pickup truck, and as they were driving, calling each other names, the pickup driver jerked the steering wheel of his truck in the direction of the motorcyclist. The motorcyclist tumbled off his bike and died. The otherwise law-abiding pickup driver, a family man with two kids and a good job, ruined his life as well the lives of both his and the motorcyclist's families. He also affected the lives of the highway patrol, medics, insurance agents, and witnesses. Had he tolerated a minor insult, his life would have been very different, and the motorcyclist would have still been alive. When we practice tolerance, we gain the insight of seeing what might have happened but didn't. The more such insight expands in us the wiser and more tolerant we become.

Just Because Things Are Out of Our Control Doesn't Mean They're Out of Control

Let's say you're at home and your car is parked outside. It's brand new, and you don't yet have insurance. Suddenly you hear tires screeching outside—a car careening around the corner. Then you hear a crash. You're sure it was your car that was hit, and you feel anxiety and experience physical symptoms: trembling, increased heart rate, perspiration, shortness of breath. When you finally come back to your senses and look outside, it turns out that it wasn't your car after all; it was your neighbors'. How do you feel now? Relieved, of course, but also sympathetic toward your neighbors.

Let's say the neighbors feel devastated when they see the state of their car, and they turn to a friend for comfort. The friend offers philosophy to help them adjust their attitude—"It's just a car; at least no people were hurt," or something like that. That's the purpose of philosophy: to objectify and then shift our perspective.

When we change our perspective, our attitude naturally shifts. It's easy to see that there is a difference between *a* car and *my* car. There are lots of cars driving around, but they're not *my* car, so I'm not concerned about them. When I think about my car, however, I care about it. I even begin to identify with it, and it becomes a part of me. For example, if someone hits my car, I might say, "You hit me."

When we become blindly attached to things, we not only suffer; we also miss the lesson. The ancient bhakti teachings say that those with an enlightened attitude learn to be objective and extract lessons from what is happening around them. What to speak of not lamenting for a car, in the *Bhagavad-gita* Krishna advises Arjuna not to lament for his body or for those of his relatives. He says that when we misidentify the body to be our self, and the things around us to

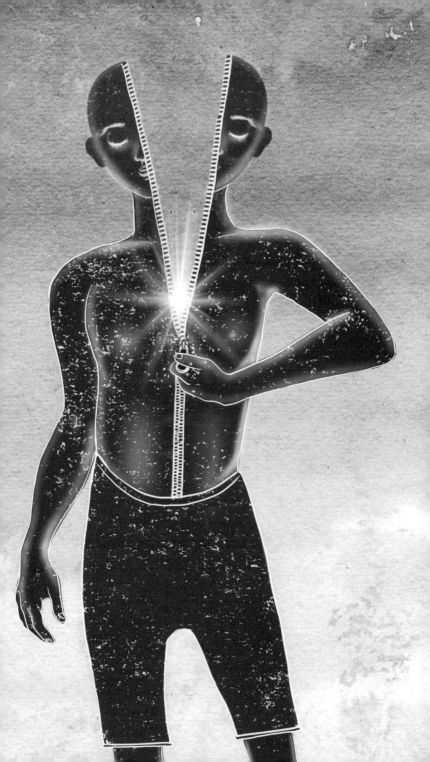

be part of us, we suffer. Our bodies are like garments. Just as we change garments at the end of the day, as non-material living entities we change bodies at the end of this life.

In life we often get the opposite of what we expect or plan for. When something goes quickly against our plans or expectations, we call it a "disaster." But just because things are out of *our* control doesn't mean they are out of control. According to *Sri Isopanishad*, the universe and everything in it is *purnam*, perfectly aligned. The way to align oneself with this universal order—despite all of life's apparent reversals—is to keep asking, "What is the lesson?"

The questions "Why me?" "Why do I deserve this?" and "Why not somebody else?" compete with "What is the lesson?" These competing questions lead us into thinking we are victims. In this way, we blame others as the cause of our woes and miss the lessons we are meant to learn. In the *Bhagavad-gita* Krishna says that the material realm is a place of miseries. He points out that in the material world difficulties come to everyone, and that we must therefore learn to tolerate them without being disturbed.

As the saying goes, "Pain is inevitable; suffering is optional." The word *suffer* comes from the root *to carry*. In other words, it is our choice whether or not to be carried away by the results of what happens to us in this material world, whether it be happiness or distress.

Getting off the Victim Wagon

When we feel victimized, the pain can be severe. Thus the bhakti teachings recognize that even as we search for the lessons or help others to do so, we may feel the pain of reversals or abuse. While seeking the lesson, therefore, we must also be compassionate—both to ourselves and to others who are suffering. Even though I am not my material body, when my finger is cut, it bleeds and hurts. When we are mistreated, we feel the pain of abuse. Looking for the lesson in what happens to us doesn't guarantee that we won't feel hurt. That's why wise people take time to solace themselves and others who feel the pain that comes from abuse, even as they ask the question, "What is the lesson?"

Maintaining a victim consciousness, however, saps our energy, is self-destructive, and debilitates our relationships. In a 2020 article in *Scientific American*, cognitive scientist Scott Barry Kaufman writes, "Those who have a perpetual victimhood mindset tend to have an external locus of control; they believe that one's life is entirely under the control of forces outside of one's self."[*] Kaufman's clinical research shows that one's mindset determines how one perceives the world. Those who compulsively identify as victims interpret life's events as assaults rather than as lessons and lose their ability to forgive. The sense of victimhood distorts

[*] https://www.scientificamerican.com/article/unraveling-the-mindset-of-victimhood/

their perspective and stifles their self-improvement.* Again, "pain is inevitable, suffering is optional."

The antidote is to replace "Why me?" with "What is the lesson?" Doing so leads us first to self-realization; then to awareness of a benevolent, higher force that is ready and willing to help; and finally, to the personal hand of the Divine, who reveals the valuable lessons we are meant to learn.

Be a Learner

This universe is designed for learning, not comfort. We are subtle spiritual beings ensconced in a material world with which we are incompatible. As oil and water never mix, similarly we never mix with the gross world of matter.

The material world is inconvenient. If we try to live a life of convenience, we'll be disappointed. If, however, we view the incidents in our lives, including the inconvenient ones, as opportunities to learn and to refine ourselves, we'll experience the exhilaration of progress. To those engaged in such a noble practice, Krishna says, "Never fear. Those who strive in this way, even imperfectly, will never be touched by misfortune." (*Bhagavad-gita* 6.40, paraphrased)

Once, there was a king named Akbar who was always accompanied by his expert and trusted chief of staff, Birbal. The king relied on Birbal's advice and depended on him to manage his affairs. One day, when Akbar was practicing martial arts with his sword, he accidentally cut off the tip of the little finger of his left hand. In pain, he inquired from Birbal, "Why has this happened to me?" Birbal replied, "It is divine arrangement." When the king heard Birbal's reply,

---

* https://www.gwern.net/docs/psychology/2020-gabay.pdf

he became angry and demanded that Birbal recant his statement. "I am the king!" he stormed. "How can such pain and suffering be 'divinely arranged'?" But Birbal held to his position, and the king, feeling insulted, ordered him put under house arrest so that he might reconsider his opinion. Birbal did not protest, and said, "This too is a divine arrangement."

A month later, the king went on an excursion into the wilderness, but because Birbal was under arrest, he could not accompany him, as he usually did on such outings. When Akbar was deep in the forest, he was captured by a tribe of tantrics—ill-advised, demented people who perform human sacrifice, thinking that the act will bring them wealth and power. As the tantrics prepared the king for sacrifice, they noticed that he was missing the tip of his little finger. Since they needed a "complete human" for a fruitful sacrifice, they released him. Having narrowly escaped death, the king rode his horse toward his palace, but all the while, he thought about Birbal—how Birbal had deemed the king's accidental cutting of his finger to be divine—and now he could see that Birbal was correct.

When he reached his kingdom, the Akbar called for Birbal to be released and brought to him. When Birbal arrived, the king embraced him and told him the story of his capture and subsequent release. "Now I can understand how it was by divine arrangement that I cut my finger," he admitted. But one thought lingered in his mind. "When I put you under house arrest," he said to Birbal, "you didn't complain, and you claimed that your arrest was also by divine arrangement. I can now understand how my situation was divinely arranged, but what about yours? You've been languishing in captivity because of my hot-headed decision."

"Please consider, Sire," Birbal replied. "If I had accompanied you on your latest excursion as I usually did, the tantrics would have sacrificed me, since my body is complete. Therefore, now we can both see that your arresting me was also divinely arranged!"

Like Birbal, those who look for the lesson in whatever happens to them will see how everything and everyone is interconnected. Instead of asking, "Why me? Why am I the victim?" ask, "What is the lesson?" When you engage in this practice, you'll find that your intelligence will be divinely empowered to find the lessons in life's events. With the question ready on your tongue, you'll climb steadily toward the high ground of self-realization, integrity, and spiritual self-esteem. Notice for yourself how simply asking "What is the lesson?" expands your consciousness. Those armed with the intention to learn and to refine themselves are ready to become master askers.

The *Gita* and other wisdom texts explain that our present life is but one in a series of lives. Each life is like a frame in a roll of cinematic film. For each of our actions, we receive a perfectly measured reaction. Whatever our present situation may be, it is the fruit of our cumulative activities from many lives. Whatever happens to us is not

arbitrary; it is a perfectly measured response to what we have already done.

When we blame God, the universe, or any entity outside ourselves, we miss the opportunity to learn and grow. When we accept the responsibility of looking for the lesson, we develop the insight and internal strength needed to embrace whatever happens to us as not only a divine intervention but also a custom-designed arrangement to help us advance. We can be victims or learners, but not both.

We are all students, and the universe is our schoolhouse. Whatever comes our way is therapy, or cosmic sensitivity training. Those who collect and apply the lessons learn to transcend all troubles and become tranquil and wise.

Eligibility for Elevation

The quintessential practice for those who seek spiritual elevation is presented in *Srimad-Bhagavatam* (10.14.8): Those who see divine, benevolent intervention in whatever happens to them, who see everything to be under the personal control of the Supreme, and who accept even adversity to be for their betterment are qualified to attain to the highest spiritual realization.

Many authors have written about how adverse times are opportunities for learning. In his book *A Walk with Prudence*, Jason Versey states, "The best education we can ever receive is from the University of Adversity. It's the only institute of learning that rewards us when we fail." Former British Prime Minister Benjamin Disraeli remarked, "There's no education like adversity." But what about the times we get what we want? In good times, fewer people ask, "Why me?" Neither do they ask, "What is the lesson?"

But those who ask these questions both in the good times and the bad reap steady rewards.

The renowned bhakti yoga teacher Narada Muni instructs spiritual seekers to learn to see loss and gain as two sides of the same karmic coin. "Loss comes of its own accord," he points out. "So too does gain. No one seeks out misery, but it finds us nonetheless. If you study the matter carefully, you will see that even when we don't exert ourselves to get material happiness, it comes to us in due course of time, just as misery does."

We learn from the *Vedas* that both happiness and misery come to us by the force of karma, the reactions to our previous activities. Some people work three jobs but never seem to get ahead financially; others don't work at all but have abundant wealth. Our material destiny finds us as handily as a calf finds its mother amidst a herd of cows.

Problems Are Gifts

The first syllable in the word *problem*, *pro*, means "forward," and *ballein* comes from an ancient word meaning "to throw." So, problems are those things that are thrown in front of us, usually when we are least expecting them, to impede us from getting something done. If we take problems as opportunities to learn, we can grow.

When problems come and we ask, "What is the lesson?" we get the courage to work through them. Each of us has the power to solve problems, and that power is activated by asking, "What is the lesson?"

The *Bhagavatam* tells the story of Bharata, a king who left his family and kingdom to meditate in the forest so that he could attain spiritual knowledge. After making great progress, one day Bharata was distracted by a deer who had prematurely delivered her fawn while attempting to escape a lion. The deer died, but the fawn lived.

Bharata saw the orphaned fawn and took it in as his own. He fed and cared for it and became attached to it. And as he gave the deer more and more attention, his meditation practice began to wane. The king gradually stopped his spiritual practices altogether.

At the end of his life, the king was so attached to the deer that when he died, it was the sole focus of his attention.

In the *Bhagavad-gita* Krishna says that what we are most absorbed in thinking of at the time of death determines the body we will get in the next life. His mind absorbed in the deer at the time of death, Bharata took his next birth as a deer. Even as a deer, however, he could remember his previous life's spiritual practices, and he continued them as best he could. So when he died and left his deer body behind, he was born as Jada Bharata, a human in the family of an educated, spiritually enriched father, and he understood how easily one can be drawn away from spiritual practice.

As Jada Bharata, he pretended to be intellectually disabled just to avoid the diversions of social intercourse, which might again sidetrack him from his spiritual goal. He even distanced himself from his own family. When his father tried to instruct him in basic matters, Jada Bharata behaved like a fool and did just the opposite of what he was told. When his father passed away, Jada Bharata left home and wandered the earth. Now he could fully absorb his mind in the Supreme, and ultimately, at the end of that life, he attained spiritual perfection, the original goal he had persued as King Bharata. His setbacks and problems had not dissuaded him from his spiritual practices; rather, they had made him evermore determined. And just as he had used his setbacks to become spiritually determined, we may follow suit.

Frustration: The Doorway to Insight

Although we don't always think of it in this way, frustration—the feeling of being upset or annoyed, especially when we can't change or achieve something—is a powerful energy that can help us to introspect. The prime cause of frustration is the feeling of losing control. When we have thoughts of how things should be when they don't go our way, we might feel anger or a lack of self-esteem. However, if we know how to utilize our frustration, it can not only help us achieve more but through introspection can also serve as a doorway to personal growth.

To open that door, we must be mindful of frustration when it arises, observing it as energy merely passing through. The more we observe it as such, the more we become aware that it is separate from us. *Srimad-Bhagavatam* (2.2.35) provides a philosophical context: "The spiritual quality of the seer is manifest in our dissatisfaction with the limited state of materially conditioned existence. That is the difference between spirit and matter." As conscious spiritual entities, we are the ones who see. A wall, pencil, or football cannot see; they are made of dead matter. We, on the other hand, are conscious, spiritual entities, and therefore, we can see. And we can specifically notice that we are not satisfied with the limited state of matter. Matter disintegrates, we don't. Matter is dead; we are alive.

When we become aware that we are frustrated, we can note why: matter and spirit are not just at odds with one another; they are polar opposites. When we become aware of this fact, we can manage our expectations. "Material happiness" is an oxymoron. As the idiom goes, "You can't get blood from a stone." Neither can we get happiness from matter.

Such awareness helps us apply a principle taught by Stephen Covey about our circle of influence and our circle of concern. Our circle of influence consists of those things in our lives that we can influence or change. Then there is the circle of concern, which is much larger. Trying to adjust matters beyond our circle of influence requires a lot of energy, clutters the mind, and closes the door to insight.

Frustration is like an unsolved puzzle. When we address it by proceeding methodically but dispassionately, staying within our circle of influence, the pieces will begin to fall into place.

Failure is the Pillar of Success

Spiritual practice isn't inaction. Neither is a spiritual practitioner immune from challenges and difficulties. Anyone who has for any reason taken to a worthy practice knows that there are always challenges and complexities. To cope with them, it's important to have a long-term, holistic perspective. Srila Prabhupada used to say that there are accidents even on royal roads. So-called failures, he wrote, "may not be detrimental; they may be the pillars of success."* Whenever I remember this, I feel both relief and a sense of determination to succeed. I hope you feel the same.

Tim Ferris, in his book *Tribe of Mentors*, lists responses by his mentors when asked, "How has a failure, or apparent failure, set you up for success later in life? Do you have a favorite failure?" One response was from Leo Babauta, the founder of Zen Habits, a website with two million readers dedicated to finding simplicity and mindfulness amidst daily chaos:

> In 2005, I was stuck—deeply in debt, overweight, addicted to junk food, no time for my family, couldn't stick to an exercise plan. I felt like an absolute failure. But this led to me researching habits and how to change them, and I put my entire being into making one single change. And then another. It led to my entire life changing, and to me helping others to change habits. It felt horrible, but it was one of the most incredible lessons of my life. The first change I made was quitting smoking, which turned out to be one of the hardest changes I've made, and I don't recommend starting with it. But I put everything I had

---

* *Light of the Bhagavata*, 43.

into it, and I learned a lot about changing habits. The next change was adding running—as a way to cope with stress after I quit smoking—and to start getting healthier. After that, I became vegetarian and started meditating.

Best-selling author Kyle Maynard, an ESPY-award-winning mixed-martial-arts athlete known as the first quadruple amputee to reach the summits of Mount Kilimanjaro and Mount Aconcagua without the aid of prosthetics, reflected on his failures:

It's almost more difficult to think of a time when an apparent failure didn't set me up for later success. Failure is inextricably connected to any major success I've ever had. My favorite failure was my earliest. My Grandma Betty had this dark green jar she used to ask me to get sugar out of, except the catch was, as an amputee, I used both arms to grip things, and I could only fit one arm inside the jar. I'd sit there for hours, repeatedly failing to balance the scoop on my one arm. I'd get it right to the edge then lose it. After 50 more tries, I'd get it back near the top before I'd lose it again. Eventually, and sometimes to my surprise, I'd succeed. It not only helped with my dexterity and focus, but it also helped build my will. The best way I can describe the feeling is a Finnish word, *sisu*—the mental strength to continue to try even after you feel you've reached the limits of your abilities. I don't think failure is sometimes part of the process—it always is. When you feel you can't go on, know that you're just getting started.

"The phoenix must burn to emerge," writes bestselling author Janet Fitch in her novel *White Oleander.* I can relate to the image of the phoenix, which cyclically expires in flame but then is reborn from the ashes. German philosopher Georg Hegel wrote, "Die to live." When our false sense of ourselves dies—when our expectations burn to ashes—we may find in the remains the indestructible sense of purpose and determination that we missed when all seemed to be going well.

There's a seed of success in failure. To water that seed is to ask, "What is the lesson?"

KEY TAKEAWAYS

- The universe is a cosmic schoolhouse.
- Just because things are out of *my* control doesn't mean they're out of control.
- Be a learner, not a victim.
- Problems are our friends.
- Failure is the pillar of success.

JOURNAL PROMPTS

Think about a challenging time in your life. It could be something with which you've been struggling, or something from your past. Jot down what happened and how it affected you emotionally. If you believe that you acted in an improper way, write that down too. Getting these things out of your mind and onto paper will give you some objective clarity.

Now ask yourself our third question: "What is the lesson?" Come up with as many different lessons as possible. Here are some examples (though you may want to hold off on reading them until you've written your own):

- I've been carrying resentment for a friend who is taking her sweet time to pay back a loan that I gave her. Lesson learned: As stated by American writer Anne Lamott, "Expectations are resentments waiting to happen."

- I got the job I've always wanted. Lesson learned: My dream job also has its faults. "Material facilities are never as good as they seem, or as bad as they seem."

If we keep asking,
"What is the best investment
of my attention right now?"
we re-align with the only point
at which we have power—
the present moment.

Question Four:
Where Am I Investing My Attention Right Now?

Our final question, "Where am I investing my attention right now?" contains two particularly important words: The verb *investing* evokes an awareness of the fact that my attention is valuable, and the noun *attention* contains the root *ten*, meaning to stretch. In attending to something, you stretch toward that object, creating a connection, like a tendon connects muscles to bones in the body. So, attention is the active direction of the mind upon some object or topic.

Giving something attention is making an investment in it, putting energy into it, and as we all know, different investments bring about different outcomes.

We Are Sparks of the Supreme

Because it is an axiomatic truth, it bears repeating that according to the yogic teachings, we, as sentient, conscious beings, are sparks of the Supreme. We have the same qualities as our divine source, just as sparks have the same quality as the fire from which they emerge. Our source is supremely conscious—omniscient, omnipotent, and omnipresent—and has unrestricted free will. As spiritual sparks, we are infinitesimal. We are minutely conscious, and our free will lies in our volition to decide where to focus. Awareness of this freedom is exhilarating: from moment to moment, we can choose where to place our attention. Or we can decline to choose and let ourselves be carried along in a kind of mass consensual trance. Many people allow preconceived notions and habits to dictate their lives, but anyone can place their attention where it can help improve their quality of life.

> Awareness of this freedom is exhilarating: from moment to moment, we can choose where to place our attention.

Rather than waking up from an absorbing dream, we sometimes resist and want to keep sleeping, even when the alarm clock rings or someone tries to wake us up. As the saying goes, it's impossible to wake up a person who is pretending to sleep. Similarly, one cannot wake a person who is dedicated to the status quo, to "ignorance as usual." You can lead a horse to water, but you can't make it drink. You can lead a man to wisdom, but you can't make him think.

Those determined to remain in their trance, to ignore the power of their own ability to choose where they place their attention, seek the association of those who support this constricted way of thinking. People addicted to drugs or engaged in other self-destructive behaviors tend to associate with people who are doing the same and avoid spending time with people who could help them give up those habits.

In a society that neglects or even outright denies spiritual values in life, destructive behavior becomes the norm. In such an environment, people who try to awaken spiritually are often maligned by those not so inclined. People dedicated to remaining in ignorance think that spiritual practitioners are foolish for wasting their time pursuing a fantasy world. Krishna therefore instructs Arjuna, "What is night for all beings is the time of awakening for the self-controlled; and the time of awakening for all beings is night for the introspective sage." (*Bhagavad-gita* 2.69)

Instead of allowing the momentum of bad habits to control our lives, we can choose to reroute our attention to thoughts and practices that uplift us. To plan one's daily activities may be practical, but more than mere time management, we need *attention* management. Ask, "Where am I investing my attention *right now?*"

Where Attention Goes, Energy Flows

The question "Where am I investing my attention right now?" is based on the idea that "Where attention goes, energy flows." Our attention is powerful. Consider a glance. Is it an electrical current? No. Is it electromagnetic? No. So, what's in a glance? Because we are spiritual entities it can be thought of like a beam of spiritual energy. When we give another person our glance, or make eye contact, something of consequence passes from us to them. The feeling one gets is different from that of being hit by the beam of a lighthouse.

When we are touched by another person's glance, we feel something beyond the touch of the material elements.

The *Bhagavad-gita* describes the body as a *yantra*, a machine made of gross and subtle material energies. Correspondingly, the mind is like the software that directs the machine. A doctor is like a mechanic, a psychologist a software engineer. But then why do we care so much about a physician's bedside manners? If we were just machines, why would we even care? Because we are *sentient* beings, and because to be sentient means to be *sensitive*, we care. So remember, your glance, your attention, has power. Regularly ask, "Where am I investing my attention right now?" and improve your life.

Our Power is Always in the Present Moment

We can only *act* in the present. But in our minds we can speculate about what is going to happen in the future. In our "mind's eye" we can see scenarios of what *might* happen. But we don't actually know what's *going* to happen; we can only deal with what is happening right now. To be effective, then, we must wisely invest our attention in the present moment. If we keep asking, "Where am I investing my attention right now?" we realign with the only point at which we have power—the present moment.

I like to call this "preparation mode." If you don't like the state you're in, go into preparation mode. That means living in the present, which automatically helps create a better future. The word *prepare* consists of the Latin *prae*, "before"; and *parare*, "to make ready." Thus, prepare means to set something in order or readiness for a particular end. For example, to cook, we have to shop, wash the ingredients, chop them up, get water boiling, and lay out the spices. You can only do these steps one at a time, and each one is as important as the other. Similarly, everything we do in life is a process, and every step of the process is important. If we take the steps that are readily available to us right now, we'll stay in the present and feel satisfied that we are accomplishing our task.

Preparation mode is a way of using our intelligence in the best way we can to engage the present moment most effectively. By preparing ourselves, we can be assured that the future is going to be better because of what we're doing now. If our minds need reassurance about the future, we can think, "I'm preparing for it right now. I'm getting ready. And it'll be better in the future. But all I can do is act in this moment."

In short, our power is always in the present moment— the platform upon which we move about this world in an enlightened way. By investing our attention in that which is most important at each moment, we can be confident that we are doing our best to accomplish our task and thus give up the burden of speculating about the future results.

From Mindlessness to Mindfulness

We often perform activities without being consciously aware of what we're doing. Have you ever met someone and just seconds later forgotten their name? The yoga texts tell us that by practice, we can learn to fix our attention. The flood of distractions in the modern age, however, makes fixing our attention difficult. Fortunately, there is a specific kind of meditation that can help develop our power of attention. It is called mantra meditation.

In mantra meditation you intone a mantra—a sacred combination of syllables, or sounds, that help uplift your mind and increase your power of attention. Repeating and listening to a mantra requires practice, but one simple direction helps: "Be aware that you're chanting." Have you ever finished a paragraph when reading a book and then realized that you have no idea what you just read? The same can happen when chanting a mantra. The cure is being vigilant to notice whether or not one is listening; and if not, to bring one's awareness back to the mantra.

The word *mantra* has two parts. *Man* means "mind," and *tra* means "to deliver." While we're reciting the mantra, our mind's tendency will be to drift away to the activities of the day, or a relationship, or an upcoming test. But by the power of the mantra, we can overcome this natural restlessness of the mind and notice that we're not obligated to attend to the myriad thoughts that stream through our minds. What's more, we can be satisfied with the luminous nature of our own consciousness.

Mantra meditation can rescue us from the river of bothersome distractions and allow us to taste the happiness of a higher perspective. When we keep asking ourselves where

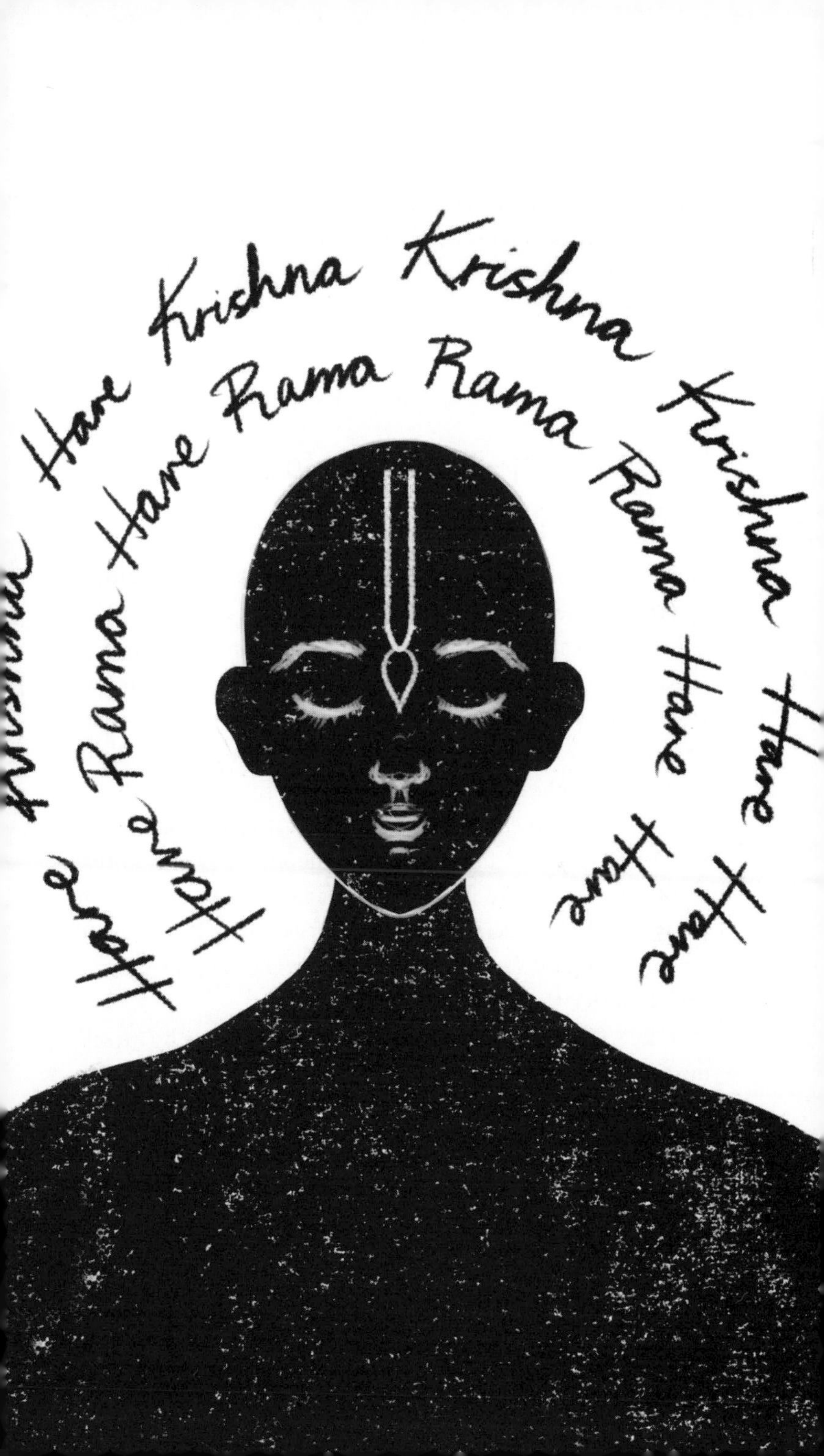
Hare Krishna Hare Krishna Krishna Krishna Hare Hare
Hare Rama Hare Rama Rama Rama Hare Hare

we are investing our attention, we come to see that we are more powerful than we might have thought. A daily practice of mantra meditation can help us not only to build our attention muscle but also to feel pleasure within. As Krishna says in the *Bhagavad-gita* (6.20–23), by this practice we can achieve the "ability to see the self by the pure mind and to relish and rejoice in the self."

Full Attention—The Secret to Quality Relationships

How we utilize our attention also affects our relationships. Improving the quality of our relationships can be as simple as giving full attention to other persons. In any relationship, our attention is our most valuable asset. How do you feel when you are trying to tell a friend something important and they only half-listen because they are busily scrolling on their phone? Not very good, right? Even a tiny diversion of attention can have a big impact. If you look at your watch when you're talking with someone, they will notice and might even take it as a sign that you don't care about what they have to say. Conversely, if we make it a point to give our friends, family, or anyone else our full attention, they'll notice that too.

Once, when I was at a conference, I was sitting by myself during a break collecting my thoughts and enjoying a little peace when a colleague approached me, enthusiastic to share his realizations from the meetings. I was tired and wasn't in the mood to talk, but then I remembered the power of attention and its consequences. So instead of giving him only half my attention, I turned my chair to face him and deliberately gave him my full attention. He was happy and expressed his gratitude, and we became friends and remain so to this day—simply because I decided to give him my full attention that one time.

The quality of attention we give to people—to all living beings—determines the quality of our relationships with them. And purposeful, undivided attention conveys the message "I care."

Deliberate to Be Deliberate

The word deliberate has two distinct yet interrelated meanings. When we deliberate, or carefully consider, these four questions, then we are empowered to be deliberate, or conscious and intentional,

> By deliberating, you become more deliberate in your actions.

in all our activities. This is one of the disciplines practiced by sadhus (the word *discipline* comes from the Latin for *learner*). The unprepared person asks, "Why me?" The sadhu asks The Four Questions.

Krishna speaks about being deliberate in the *Bhagavad-gita* (2.41): "Those who are on this path are resolute in purpose, and their aim is one. O beloved child of the Kurus, the intelligence of those who are irresolute is many-branched." Their aim is one, *ekeha*. The opposite, *avyavasayinam*, means *not* to have a purpose, not to have a clear idea of where we're going. In this case, our attention becomes *bahu-sakha*, "unlimitedly branched." Our purpose, then, is not fixed because we have no clear idea of where we're going. Once you deliberate on your purpose and develop a clear idea of your goals, you become more deliberate in the things you do to achieve those goals. By becoming resolute in purpose, you intentionally learn to invest your attention, which leads to being more efficient and feeling more fulfilled.

Setting Our Purpose

The wisdom literatures recommend that we set a *sankalpa*, a purpose or intention, before starting anything important. The word *sankalpa* means to solemnly formulate one's intention, especially verbally or in writing. A *sankalpa* can also be called an affirmation—a positive, self-directed statement that affirms our goal. Sadhus typically verbalize their *sankalpas* first thing in the morning upon awakening. One such *sankalpa* is a verse that says, "I am not my body or mind; I am a spiritual being, a servant of the servant of the Supreme." Another way to align ourselves in purpose before we start an important task is to recite a sacred mantra, a phrase that contains names of the Supreme.

If we have an affirmation ready—a sacred mantra or other prayers or specific intentions—and get into the habit of speaking them aloud to ourselves, we deliberately remind ourselves of our purpose before starting anything. And this sets us off in the direction we want to go.

Return on Attention (ROA)

We are investors. Economic theory calls money "dollar votes." But what is our most important investment, and where does our vote count the most? The answer is, where we invest our attention.

We hear about maximizing our ROI, return on investment. But I like the term ROA, return on attention. Just as some monetary investments are more lucrative than others, some investments of our attention yield greater results than others. The word *investment* implies that we are contributing toward achieving a greater goal. When we invest our attention regularly to a worthy cause over time, the results can be extraordinary.

When we invest our attention only in impermanent things that are here today, gone tomorrow—like our bodies, our money, our possessions—we get diminishing returns. But if we make even a small daily investment in ourselves as spiritual beings through spiritual practices, we invest in the permanent, the eternal, and over time that investment compounds and multiplies exponentially. Albert Einstein called compound interest the "eighth wonder of the world." Spiritual practice yields compounding wealth—invaluable qualities like patience, satisfaction, fearlessness, and so on—that never diminish. In the *Gita* (2.40), Krishna says this about spiritual practice: "In this endeavor there is no loss or diminution, and a little advancement on this path can protect one from the most dangerous type of fear."

I had a profound experience once in Washington DC, when I was introduced to a gentleman who was dying. He had never been very serious about spiritual life, but when he became terminally ill, and as death approached, he felt an urge to use the remaining days he had to make up for time wasted. He asked me to sit next to him, grabbed my hand, and asked me for guidance.

In his last few days, he took my advice and started to practice mantra meditation and to pray. I visited him daily, and from his bed he told me that he wanted to donate money to a local spiritual community. As he was writing a check, however, he turned to me with a pained look and said, "All my life I have been so absorbed in earning money, growing my investments, and keeping the profits all for myself. It's hard at this point for me to give even a small portion of it away. I'm not used to this."

I saw the incident as an instructive metaphor for spiritual practice. The eighth chapter of the *Bhagavad-gita* places great emphasis on our leaving the world in the right state of mind. As Krishna tells Arjuna, the way we invest our energy during our lives will determine our consciousness at the end. A selfless, giving heart is developed by investing one's attention in metaphysical practices that increase the willpower to overcome the challenges of the material body and mind. But again, no shortcuts exist; to overcome material challenge requires practice. Only by developing *yoga-balena*, the strength that comes from connecting to the Supreme, can we attain our highest ROA at the end of life. And, as we read in the *Gita* (8.6), your ROA determines your future—how you invest your attention in this life will determine your destination in the next.

Direct Your Attention Wisely

As the old saying goes, if you chase two rabbits, you won't catch either one. Our power lies in our ability to focus our attention in the right place. When we do this, we get the highest return from life. This is an essential teaching of bhakti. With so many distractions and options, we must be alert to direct our attention to what really matters.

Krishna explains to Arjuna that whatever we immerse ourselves in becomes part of us: "While contemplating (*dhyayato*) the objects of the senses (*visayan*), a person develops attachment for them (*sanga*)." (*Bhagavad-gita* 2.62) This is how we become intimately connected to the world: we feel that a house, a car, a family, a pet—or even our own bodies—are a part of us; *dhyayato* means "to dwell on or contemplate," and *visayan* refers to the all the things that vie for our attention. If I dwell on a sense object with the desire to own, control, and enjoy it, then by the power of my consciousness and by the way I've directed my attention, I develop a *sanga*, an attachment. The word *sanga* comes from the Sanskrit root *sanj*, which means "to stick together."

I might look at a bicycle and think, "I just *have* to have that bike! I'd look great riding around on it. Of course, I'd have to lock it up so no one could steal it." All these thoughts race through my mind. And by this process of *dhyayato*, or contemplation, I identify myself with the bike. I develop a *sanga* with it. I don't have to officially own an object to become attached to it, and for it to become a part of my life.

Many people become attached to sports teams. They watch a team and let it absorb their consciousness—"I'm a fan of such-and-such." When their team wins, they're ecstatic; when it loses, they're morose. They've made a *sanga* with the team: it has become a part of who they are, and their happiness is tied to its success. But when we attach ourselves to a team or a concept or an ideology, or to any material object, wanting to enjoy or to control it by making it "ours"—we pay the price, just as one pays rent on a dwelling.

On one side, people who invest their attention in the aimless scrolling of random social media posts, breaking news, or pornography soon find their minds attached to those sounds and images. The penalty is acute anxiety, depression, mental discord—a poor ROA, to say the least. They pay interest and fees on their greed and unhealthy cravings for temporary objects. And when those cravings aren't fulfilled, they become angry. "From such attachment," Krishna tells Arjuna, "lust develops, and from lust frustration and anger arise, which leads to bewilderment of memory."

On the other side, those who invest their attention wisely, regulating their senses in spiritual practice, reap the dividends of *yajna* (sacrifice): wisdom and a peaceful mind and heart. Chanting sacred mantras and hearing from the ancient wisdom texts both give healthy returns on attention.

What you direct your attention to is vital. Where attention goes, energy flows.

The Main Thing is to Keep the Main Thing the Main Thing

We learn from the wisdom texts that the universe is comprised of two primary energies: inert matter and the conscious spirit (*atma*). In the *Gita* (7.4–5) Krishna lists the inert material elements: earth, water, fire, air, ether, mind, intelligence, and false ego. Superior to these, he says, are the conscious living entities whose consciousness animates this inert matter. The conscious living entity is covered by a gross and subtle body. The gross body is made of earth, water, fire, air, and ether (space). The subtle body consists of mind, intelligence, and false ego. The body is therefore made up of a hierarchy of gross and subtle matter: lowest are the senses, above the senses is the mind, above the mind is the intelligence. It is the superior energy (*atma*) that activates and animates the material body, gross and subtle. We are the *atma*, or the conscious self, which is categorically different from and superior to all these gradations of gross and subtle matter.

In the same vein, Patanjali Muni in his *Yoga-sutras* contrasts the *seer*—the conscious being—with the body and mind. Without the conscious being, the body and mind are like dark stained-glass windows. But when the superior conscious being is within, the body and mind are illuminated and appear to be alive.

In *The Seven Habits of Highly Effective People* Steven Covey writes, "The main thing is to keep the main thing the main thing." But what *is* the main thing? And where *should* we put our attention? Where will we get the best ROA? First, by self-realization, or perceiving that we are different from our material body. Second, by meditation on the Supreme. The yoga wisdom texts say that Krishna not only pervades the universe but is also personally present as the "Superself" within the heart of every individual living being. The wisdom literatures say that the *atma*, or individual conscious being, and the Superspirit are like two birds living in the same tree. Patanjali Muni says that a yogi can at once bypass the lower stages of self-realization by meditating on the Superself. In the *Gita* we also learn that the best of all yogis is the one who, out of love, bhakti, fixes their attention on the Superself.

Your Level of Contentment Depends on Your Content

The wisdom texts explain that the subtle, or psychological, body as described above comprises three elements—the mind (*manas*), the intellect (*buddhi*), and false ego (*ahankara*).

INTELLECT

MIND FALSE EGO

These elements combine to form a sort of digital cloud, or storage space. Impressions from our senses are stored in our subtle body. These impressions, called *samskaras*, are latent, but can be brought to our awareness, just as we bring up an old photo on Google Drive. All our sensory experiences—in this life and in previous lifetimes—are stored within the subtle body, which we take with us when we go to a new gross body. That's why every one of us has unique predispositions and natural talents which were developed even before we were born.

Every impression we take in through our senses affects what we do, say, and think. In other words, the way we move about this world has consequences—sequences that happen as a result of our activities. This is what is called karma: I do something, and there is a consequence, a resultant sequence of events that unfolds over time.

Ancient yogis were extremely careful about what they allowed into their consciousness through the senses. They didn't allow degrading impressions to nest within their minds. In this regard, as noted by one commentator, the yogis realized that their minds were as sensitive as eyeballs. Consider how the eyes are two of the most delicate surfaces on the body, irritated by the touch of even a tiny strand of hair. Meditators and yogis today retain an awareness that whatever we allow to enter our consciousness will remain and have a lasting effect. They're careful, therefore, about what they allow to enter and are deliberate about keeping their minds free of "rubbish."

Fortify Yourself—Cultivate Inner Happiness

Still, as long as we are in this world, we have to work and interact with it. It's hardly practical, or desirable, to shut out or ignore the world or the loving relationships we have with the people in it; nor is it possible to completely avoid environments fraught with negativity and lower vibrations. So how does one fortify oneself from being influenced by negative energies?

Those who daily engage in spiritual practice are content because they enjoy pleasure within. They understand that everything has a relationship with the Supreme and that everything is meant to be used in service to the Supreme. With such a service attitude, feeling full in themselves, they move about the world without being disturbed by even the most agitating sights and sounds. In contrast, those lacking such inner fulfillment are like consumers who shop when they are hungry or restless. Bewildered by unlimited choices, they indiscriminately buy what they don't need, often things that are bad for them.

Persons who daily, especially as the dawn breaks, connect with the Divine through bhakti yoga feel contentment and inner strength. When we meditate on sublime mantras, read elevated books like the *Bhagavad-gita*, hear from sadhus, and dedicate our work to the Supreme, we become fulfilled. Armed with such a higher taste, we naturally forego the nonessential and are able to make wise, discriminate choices.

I recently attended a memorial service for one of my best friends from high school. After the ceremony, I conversed with the other attendees, some

INNER
fulfillment

INNER
Hunger

of whom were drinking wine. I noticed that the more they drank the less able they were to understand subtle concepts. For example, one of my old high school teachers, knowing that I had joined a monastery after my junior year, asked me about the course of my life and the philosophy I was following. I explained to her the concept that we are not our physical bodies but spiritual beings. Initially, she had a keen interest and was beginning to resonate with the concept, but the more wine she consumed the less she could process our conversation. She had embraced the lower energy of the alcohol. I was simply observing and marveling at how this lower energy was working. I thought, "Be careful what you feed your mind."

Ricky and His Mice

As the saying goes, "We are what we eat." Similarly, the mind transforms according to what we feed it. For his fifth-grade science-fair project, another of my childhood friends, Ricky Masanno, wanted to test the importance of what we eat. He fed one mouse junk food and another mouse the same amount of nutritious food. After three months, the mouse who ate the junk food looked like a skinny runt, the well-fed one like an Olympic athlete. That's how the mind is. If we feed our mind with low vibrations—negative thoughts and petty desires—it becomes malnourished, but if we fortify it by adopting a healthy spiritual diet, regularly feeding it spiritual sound in the form of mantra and wisdom, the mind becomes strong.

Get Absorbed in Transcendental Topics

One of the great secrets of refining the intelligence is that we all have the innate ability to choose what we allow to enter our subtle body through the senses. The wisdom literatures describe a hierarchy of three modes of nature, called *gunas*, which produce the unlimited varieties of forms that condition us in various ways. Just as an artist, or a color printer, combines the three basic colors (blue, red, and yellow) to produce unlimited colors, the modes of nature, which are like three-dimensional colors, mix to create all the material forms of this world. These modes are always in flux, and the mind is dominated at every moment by a particular mode, based on the things we choose to feed it; in this way, a proportionate level of intellectual refinement is established accordingly. The *Gita* (13.22) explains that our involvement in good or bad situations in the world is due to our association with material nature. How we invest our attention determines our direction and our fortune. Therefore the mind must be refined so that it can be a proper medium to absorb enlightened thoughts. In another verse the *Gita* says that one's mind can be one's best friend or worst enemy. Obviously, it's preferable to make the mind our best friend.

The Three Modes of Nature

The wisdom texts explain the details of how the three modes of nature affect us. Goodness (*sattva guna*) is the modality of light, virtue, wisdom, truth, and clarity. When we live a sattvic way of life, we remain determined in the face of success or failure, because we work from a sense of duty, not for material gain. Furthermore, we are open to hear spiritual topics, and we naturally see the unity of living beings. In *sattva* we are truthful, tolerant, self-controlled, peaceful, and content.

In the mode of goodness, we see that everything has the same original source and that we are all part of that source. The *Rig Veda* explains this sattvic perspective: "Truth is one, though the wise refer to it in various ways."

Persons in *sattva guna* have unbreakable firmness of purpose because they're not attached to the results of their work. They also feel the natural happiness that comes from doing selfless service as an offering to the Supreme. Thus, they work more conscientiously than a person motivated by greed and get higher quality results.

The mode beneath *sattva* is *rajas*, or passion. The *Bhagavad-gita* lists the symptoms of a person influenced by *rajas*: attachment to trivial things, intense endeavor, and uncontrollable desire and hankering for name, fame, and material achievements. Those

PASSION   GOODNESS

IGNORANCE

driven by *rajas* see only the superficial bodily differences of living beings. They are prejudiced against and antagonistic toward those who look different or think differently from them. There are all kinds of "isms" in the world—racism, nationalism, speciesism, and so on—and they all stem from *rajas*, which puts us at irreconcilable odds with one another. Persons in *rajas* are attached to the results of their work. They are greedy and affected by success and failure. Their determination wavers: If rewarded, they're happy; if not, they quit.

The lowest of the three modes is *tamas*, or ignorance. The symptoms of *tamas* are laziness, cheating, foolishness, procrastination, fearfulness, and moroseness. Those influenced by *tamas* are asleep spiritually. Their minds are attracted by and become attached to dogmatic theories based on fear, speculation, and conspiracies. They are infamous for their expertise at insulting others.

Know Your Modes

A trained physician can both diagnose a patient's disease and predict its future symptoms. Similarly, someone who is aware of the symptoms of the three modes of nature and has studied their effects can also predict the attitudes and proclivities of a person affected by the various combinations of the modes.

For example, a person affected by *tamas* will procrastinate and tend to have a fatalistic outlook on life: "I'm no good. Everyone hates me. I may as well not try." A person in rajas is driven to get ahead in the material world and constantly thinks about getting more things and strives for a better career and a more prestigious position. Even after capturing their prized goals, however, those in *rajas* are not satisfied; they're prodded by *rajas* to want more and more. And their determination fluctuates between hot and cold. They are driven by material desires but are inevitably frustrated, whether they achieve their goals or not.

For those who wish to learn the science of nature's modes in more detail, Krishna gives an even more comprehensive list of their symptoms in *Srimad-Bhagavatam* (11.25.2-5):

Mind and sense control, tolerance, discrimination, sticking to one's prescribed duty, truthfulness, mercy, careful study of the past and future, satisfaction in any condition, generosity, renunciation of sense gratification, faith in the spiritual master, being embarrassed by one's own improper action, charity, simplicity, humbleness, and self-satisfaction are qualities of the mode of goodness (*sattva*).

Material desire, great endeavor, audacity, dissatisfaction even in gain, false pride, praying for material advancement, considering oneself different and better than others, sense gratification, rash eagerness to fight, a fondness for hearing oneself praised, the tendency to ridicule others, advertising one's own prowess, and justifying one's actions by one's strength are qualities of the mode of passion (*rajas*).

Intolerant anger, stinginess, speaking whimsically, violent hatred, living as a parasite, hypocrisy, fatigue, quarrel, lamentation, delusion, unhappiness, depression, sleeping too much, false expectations, fear, foolishness, and laziness constitute the major qualities of the mode of ignorance (*tamas*).

When we are predominantly influenced by a particular mode of nature, we become conditioned by it and therefore seek pleasure through objects and concepts in the same mode, as if against our will.

The practice of bhakti yoga upgrades our conditioning so that we can develop a sattvic mindset. When our mind is in the clarity of goodness, we can reach for an even higher goal—to transcend all three modes of nature and reach pure consciousness, the spiritual platform. As Krishna tells Arjuna in the *Gita* (14.26), "One who engages in full devotional service, unfailing in all circumstances, at once transcends the modes of material nature and thus comes to the level of brahman." So just by doing bhakti yoga, following the sadhus, we can rise above the modes of nature and come to our pure, spiritual state of existence.

The consequence of misplacing our attention is mentioned in *Srimad-Bhagavatam* (11.2.37): *isad apetasya viparyayo 'smrtih. Isad apetasya* means "to turn away from the Supreme," and *viparyayo 'smrtih* means "forgetting our constitutional nature as spiritual beings." In other words, as we turn away from the light of our spiritual identity in relationship with the Supreme and seek happiness independently, we find only frustration in the darkness of the lower modes of nature.

The more we allow ourselves to soak up the lower modes of material nature, the more we are affected by them and the more life becomes agitating and bewildering. But we don't have to subject ourselves to such bedlam. Fortunately, we can "reprogram" our lives, just as software engineers can write new codes to override dated or ineffective ones. The yoga process empowers us to overwrite codes that impel us to think and act in ways detrimental to our well-being. *Srimad-Bhagavatam* teaches how to live without being touched by lower material influences. How? By properly investing our attention in spiritual practices like working for a higher purpose, mantra meditation, bonding with sadhus, and hearing sacred texts with rapt attention.

Another way to invest our attention properly goes back to our second question, "How can I be of service?" As Srila Prabhupada writes, "[The mind] should be so trained that it can be always thinking of doing good for others." (*Bhagavad-gita* 17.16, purport) As we redirect our attention toward spiritual practices and devotional service, the binding ropes of lower energies begin to loosen.

It isn't always easy to invest our attention in ways we would like, especially considering how easy it is to become even inadvertently diverted by unhealthy addictions. In the 2019 article "The Neurobiology of Addiction," published in the *Annals of the New York Academy of Sciences* journal, researchers describe how addictive substances or stimuli hijack the brain's dopamine system. Dopamine is a neurotransmitter that is involved in the sensation of pleasure. Addiction causes the brain to release unnaturally high amounts of dopamine, which causes us to identify the object of addiction with the feeling of pleasure.*

How, then, can we change our habits and overcome degrading addictions? We must practice. The bhakti yoga texts recognize that it is our nature as sentient beings to be strongly attached to something or someone. This is the living condition. The practice of bhakti yoga transfers our attachments to transcendental topics, activities, and association. In *Srimad-Bhagavatam* 1.5.33, the master-teacher Narada presents this principle: "Does not a thing, applied therapeutically, cure a disease which was caused by that very same thing?" Because we are naturally attracted to things that bring us happiness, the process of bhakti shows

---

* https://www.ncbi.nlm.nih.gov/pmc/articles/PMC6767400/

us which things to transfer our attachment to for lasting pleasure. As we realize for ourselves the superior happiness we derive from performing devotional service, we naturally give up the taste we've acquired through association with the lower modes of nature—without artificial or unnatural restraints. For example, the process of bhakti is full of activities that people already enjoy in their lives: singing, dancing, looking at beautiful art, being with high-minded people, and tasting delicious food. In bhakti yoga, all these pleasures are positively purifying because they are enjoyed in association with the Supreme.

Ascending, Then Transcending, The Three Modes

If our way of life keeps us involved in passion and ignorance, we will be swept away by these lower modes. But, again, remember that we have the choice of where to place our awareness, and where attention goes, energy flows. At first, we may not always be able to make the right choice, but when we act with awareness of the consequences of superior and inferior choices, we begin to improve our investment of attention. We can't rise any higher than our priorities in life, and to upgrade our priorities we need deliberation and good association. From there, through the practice of bhakti yoga, we can direct our attention toward service to the Divine.

Our original nature is to be truly happy by experiencing transcendental pleasure. It's simply a matter of knowing where that pleasure resides and applying the right principles. The first principle is to ask, "Where am I investing my attention right now?"

One who has transcended the modes is consistently happy for no apparent reason—simply because that's the nature of our original pure consciousness. Such persons are also happy because they have a healthy attitude toward possessions and relationships—car, house, family, friends, and so on—in that they appreciate them as gifts given to them by the Supreme, the source of everything.

Practice Mantra Meditation

To focus our attention, the yoga wisdom texts recommend the process of mantra meditation—fixing one's mind on a kind of potent sound. Authentic meta-physical sound vibrations may seem like any other sound—just a combination of syllables—but Vedic mantras originate from outside of the material world. They are eternal mantras passed down by generations of sadhus. These authorized mantras lift us above the influence of the three material modes. When we practice mantra meditation, the sound we produce is not inert material sound but tran- 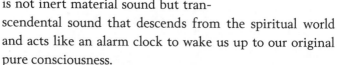 scendental sound that descends from the spiritual world and acts like an alarm clock to wake us up to our original pure consciousness.

There are other forms of meditation, like staring at a flame or concentrating on the breath, but mantra meditation, which is most recommended by authentic wisdom texts for the age in which we live, has a special potency which other methods lack. The scientific principle of excitation helps to explain why mantra meditation is so potent. In physics, excitation is defined as the introduction of a higher energy to something situated in a lower state. When that higher energy touches an object of lower energy, it elevates the lower object to a higher state. Likewise, Vedic mantras energize us and bring us to a higher awareness, bringing us eventually to our original consciousness, which is eternal, full of knowledge, and blissful.

In summary, mantra meditation frees our mind from material absorption, the cause of all perplexity and anxiety, and opens up a world of spiritual knowledge and happiness. It gradually awakens direct perception of our original consciousness and brings us back to our real life. Material pleasures are temporary at face value, but compared to spiritual pleasure, they're but a flash in the pan—utterly insignificant.

The *Maha-mantra*

The mantra most highly recommended by the *Vedas* and sadhus alike is called the *maha-mantra*, the "great mantra for deliverance":

> *Hare Krishna Hare Krishna*
> *Krishna Krishna Hare Hare*
> *Hare Rama Hare Rama*
> *Rama Rama Hare Hare*

The *Kali-santarana Upanisad* says that by chanting the *maha-mantra* one can overcome the myriad obstacles to spiritual advancement—distractions, procrastination, bad habits, and so on—that we inevitably face in the modern age.

The chanting of the *maha-mantra* benefits not only those who recite it but also others who hear it, thus initiating a purifying chain reaction that improves the world's atmosphere. Transcendental sound reverses the dark influences created by all the lower, defective sounds that pervade and degrade the world. Who hasn't noticed the unsettled state of the world these days—the epidemics of envy, sectarianism, hate, and violence?

The Power of Spiritual Sound Vibration

Every physical particle in the universe—each cell in one's body—has a particular vibration, and all material manifestations are held together by vibrational forces.* According to Vedic thought, we, as conscious entities, are part of a higher energy, above this world of inert matter.

Our good fortune comes from connecting to this higher energy, which is perfect, eternal, and blissful. Our failures come from investing our sense of worth and happiness in the material realm, which is temporary and full of misery.

When we invest our attention in listening to sounds tinged by the three modes, we tie ourselves to the material realm and its miseries of birth, death, old age, and disease. Hearing transcendental sound elevates us above matter, allowing us to not only perceive our spiritual nature but also to be in direct contact with our original divine source, Krishna. Srila Prabhupada describes the benefits of listening to these sounds:

> As living spiritual souls, we are all originally Krishna conscious entities, but due to our association with matter since time immemorial, our consciousness is now polluted by the material atmosphere. In this

---

* https://www.pbs.org/wgbh/nova/article/the-good-vibrations-of-quantum-field-theories/

polluted concept of life, we are all trying to exploit the resources of material nature, but actually we are becoming more and more entangled in her complexities. This illusion is called *maya*, or [the] hard struggle for existence over the stringent laws of material nature. This illusory struggle against the material nature can at once be stopped by revival of our Krishna consciousness. Krishna consciousness is not an artificial imposition on the mind. This consciousness is the original energy of the living entity. When we hear the transcendental vibration, this consciousness is revived.*

The best way to invoke internal and external peace, therefore, is to individually and collectively hear and chant transcendental sounds that culminate in the *maha-mantra*, which harmonizes our energy with the Supreme:

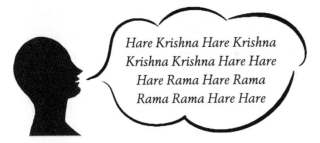

*Hare Krishna Hare Krishna
Krishna Krishna Hare Hare
Hare Rama Hare Rama
Rama Rama Hare Hare*

The *maha-mantra* contains three words: *Hare, Krishna,* and *Rama. Hare* refers to the energy of our energetic Divine Source. *Krishna* is that energetic Divine Source of all energies. *Rama* means the wellspring of eternal happiness. Srila Prabhupada taught that the *maha-mantra* is a prayerful call:

---

* "Kṛṣṇa Consciousness," spoken by Srila Prabhupada on *The Happening* album, 1966.

"Oh energy of the Supreme, Oh Supreme, please engage me in your service."

The *maha-mantra* is uniquely potent because the names of the Divine are non-different from the Divine. Since Krishna is absolute, all his features, such as his name and form, are also absolute. By reciting the *maha-mantra*, we come into direct contact with him, our Supreme Source.

Fix Your Attention by Making a Vow

Since the quality of our determination comes from the material modes we have acquired, those who want to remain steady in their determination should cultivate the mode of goodness. When our food, association, music—all our choices—are in goodness, we naturally feel determined.

One way to be fixed in goodness is to make a vow. The mind is constantly running off in all directions, and a vow can help us fix and properly invest our attention. For instance, we can make a vow to chant a certain number of mantras every day. This is called *sankhya-purvaka*, which means "numerical strength." If you set a goal for the number of mantras you recite every day and stick to it, the effect will be more substantial, similar to how a doctor might prescribe a medicine and say, "Here's ten days' worth. Take two a day, and make sure you take them all even if you start to feel better."

Setting a numerical vow for our practices helps tame the mind, because once we make a vow, the regularity of our practice becomes fixed and not dependent on the mind's whims. Some days, when we are in tune, we'll think, "This vow was a great idea," and we'll be happy and inspired to complete the practice. Other days, our mind may think, "I'm not really into this," but because of our vow, we'll be able to stick to our practice. When the mind is defiant, the intelligence kicks in and says, "We made this vow for a reason, and we're going to stick to it." By keeping a vow, we develop spiritual strength, which enables us to resist the mind's various whimsies and temptations.

Be Consistent

Consistency is more important than quantity, so it's best to start with a vow we can maintain, however small it may be. If we stay consistent over time, both the quantity and quality of our practice will improve. When we add even a small amount of yogurt to a large pot of milk in a favorable environment, the entire pot of milk transforms into yogurt overnight. Consistent bhakti practice is like that drop of yogurt—adding even a little to our daily schedule will not only improve the quality of each day but will eventually spiritualize our entire life.

KEY TAKEAWAYS

- Where attention goes, energy flows.

- By deliberating, you become more deliberate in your actions.

- Invest your attention wisely to maximize your return on attention (ROA).

- Your level of contentment depends on your content.

- Practice mantra meditation to transcend the material modes and feel inner happiness.

JOURNAL PROMPTS

1. List the ten things you spend the most time doing.

2. Figure out which ones take up the most time.

3. Decide which ones you'd like to invest more (or less) time in.

4. Make a tweak to your schedule to improve your ROA, starting today.

Conclusion

Practice Asking

Now we have The Four Questions: 1) What is my purpose? 2) How may I be of service? 3) What is the lesson? and 4) Where am I investing my attention right now? But it takes practice to develop the habit of asking them, just as it takes practice to learn to play a musical instrument. With practice of any discipline, come obstacles. These obstacles are opportunities to ask relevant questions about how to proceed.

At first, the discipline needed to ask The Four Questions may seem challenging. But it's worth the effort. It can help to write them down and keep them with you. Someone recently told me that he found the questions to be "amazing tools" that helped him build a stronger foundation for his life and gave him a deeper sense of purpose. He said, "These four questions have ignited in me a greater sense of confidence in all my endeavors and a deeper spiritual outlook."

By preparing ourselves to ask the right questions, in times of stress we'll have a rope with which to pull ourselves out of the quicksand of frustration and anxiety. Those who practice asking The Four Questions grow spiritually. The questions give rise to the realization that we are spiritual—not merely physical, mental, or intellectual—beings. The more we ask them, the more we align ourselves with the highest energies of the universe. Asking the right questions really does bring us the answers that enrich our lives.

As humans, we can adapt. Our minds are flexible and can adjust to the world's ever-changing circumstances. In the bhakti practice, the primary way by which  we adapt is by becoming master askers. The Four Questions are like an existential repositioning system. When we ask them, we facilitate growth in all areas of our lives. We're not going to know all the answers—we never could; the world is fast-moving and vast. But we can become life-long learners.

The Four Questions are universal. They are applicable in any spiritual practice and all aspects of our lives. The bhakti texts explain that when we regulate ourselves and develop a spiritual routine in our lives, we gain freedom. It may seem paradoxical that the more disciplined we become, the freer we are. But the process of sincere spiritual practice frees us from misconceptions and illusions and allows us to follow our true nature and relish our inherent joy.

Thank you, dear reader, for reading this book. May The Four Questions guide us as we work together to do good for ourselves and the world. May we ask our way to clarity and, ultimately, to an ever-stronger connection to Krishna, our Divine Source.

Glossary

Akincana–one who possesses nothing in the material world.

Arjuna–one of the five Pandava brothers; Sri Krishna became his chariot driver during the battle of Kurukshetra and spoke *Bhagavad-gita* to him.

Ashtanga–the eight-step process of meditation, beginning with sitting postures and breath control, and culminating with realization of the Supreme in the heart.

Athato Brahma Jijnasa–the first verse of the *Vedanta-sutras*, which means "Now is the time to inquire about the absolute truth."

Atma–the individual living entity, who is an eternal minute part of the Supreme.

Bhagavad-gita–the paramount wisdom literature of the Vedic tradition, embodying the teachings of Sri Krishna to His devotee Arjuna, and expounding devotion to the Supreme as both the principal means and the ultimate end of spiritual perfection.

Bhagavatam–another name for the *Srimad-Bhagavatam*.

Bhakti Tirtha Swami–a spiritual leader and a disciple of Srila A. C. Bhaktivedanta Swami Prabhupada, known for his teachings on Bhakti Yoga.

Bhakti Yoga–the practice of devotional service to the Supreme.

Bhaktivinoda Thakura–(1874-1915) the "grandfather" of the International Society for Krishna Consciousness; the spiritual master of Srila A. C. Bhaktivedanta Swami Prabhupada.

Bharata–a great devotee of the Supreme who because of neglect of spiritual duties took birth as a deer; in his following birth, as a human, he attained perfection.

Caitanya-caritamrta–Krishnadasa Kaviraja Goswami's presentation of the life and philosophy of Sri Chaitanya Mahaprabhu.

Chaitanya–refers to Sri Chaitanya Mahaprabhu, the incarnation of the Supreme Personality of Godhead, disguised as His own devotee, who descended to teach love of Krishna through the process of congregational chanting of the holy names of the Supreme.

Dharma–the eternal function of the living entity.

Gita–short for *Bhagavad-gita*.

Gunas–the three modes, or qualities, of material nature–goodness, passion, and ignorance.

ISKCON–the International Society for Krishna Consciousness, a global movement founded by Srila A. C. Bhaktivedanta Swami Prabhupada to teach Bhakti Yoga.

Jada Bharata–the name of Bharata after his second rebirth as a human, which occurred after his giving up the body of a deer.

Jnana Yoga–the path of spiritual realization through a speculative philosophical search for truth.

Kali-santarana Upanishad–an ancient wisdom text that notes the Hare Krishna maha-mantra as the principal spiritual practice for the present Age.

Karma Yoga–the path of realizing the Supreme through dedicating the fruits of one's work to the Supreme.

Krishna–the Supreme Personality of Godhead, appearing in His original, two-armed form, which is the origin of all His other forms and incarnations.

Maha-mantra–the great chanting for deliverance–Hare Krishna, Hare Krishna, Krishna Krishna, Hare Hare/ Hare Rama, Hare Rama, Rama Rama, Hare Hare.

Mantra–a syllable, word, or verse with special spiritual potency chanted or meditated upon to invoke spiritual understanding and realization.

Maya–the material energy; the illusory energy of the Supreme that deludes the living entities into forgetfulness of their real, spiritual nature.

Niyamagraha–The tendency to either adhere fanatically to, or to neglect the rules and regulations of spiritual practice.

Patanjali Muni–the author of the original yoga system.

Purnam–"complete."

Queen Kunti–the mother of the Pandavas and the aunt of Krishna.

Rajas–the material mode of passion, characterized by materialistic endeavor and the desire for sense gratification.

Rama–(1) a name of Sri Krishna meaning "the source of all pleasure"; (2) Sri Ramachandra, an incarnation of Krishna as a perfect righteous king.

Ramayana–a Vedic epic narrating the life of Sri Ramachandra.

Rupa Goswami–the chief of the six Vaishnava spiritual masters who directly followed Sri Chaitanya Mahaprabhu and systematically presented His teachings.

Sadhana–the practice of a discipline, like yoga.

Sadhu–one who exemplifies a practice.

Sadhya–the goal of a practice.

Samsara–the cycle of repeated birth and death in the material world.

Samskaras–impressions or imprints left on the mind by past actions or experiences.

Sanatana Goswami–one of the six Vaishnava spiritual masters who directly followed Sri Chaitanya Mahaprabhu and systematically presented His teachings.

Sanatana-dharma–the transcendental religion that is the eternal function of the living entity.

Sanga–spiritual association.

Sankalpa–the declaration of one's intention.

Sankhya-purvaka–"numerical strength" gained by deliberately counting one's spiritual practices.

Sattva–the material mode of goodness, characterized by purity, satisfaction and peacefulness.

Sita–the wife of Sri Ramachandra, an incarnation of Krishna.

Sri Ishopanishad–one of the principal *Upanishads*.

Srila A.C. Bhaktivedanta Swami Prabhupada–The Founder-Acharya of the International Society for Krishna Consciousness (ISKCON).

Srila–a title of respect.

Srimad-Bhagavatam–the *Purana*, or history, written by Vyasadeva specifically to give a deep understanding of Krishna.

Sukadeva–the sage who spoke *Srimad-Bhagavatam* to King Parikshit just prior to the king's death.

Tamas–the material mode of nature, characterized by ignorance, lethargy and madness

Upanishads–the philosophical division of the *Vedas*, meant for bringing a student closer to understanding the personal nature of the Absolute Truth.

Vedas–the four wisdom literatures, *Rg*, *Yajur*, *Sama* and *Atharva*, and in a broader sense, including the *Upanishads* and *Vedanta-sutra*.

Vedanta-sutra–Vyasadeva's summary of the theistic philosophy of the Vedic literature, written in the form of concise codes.

Vedic–pertaining to a culture in which all aspects of human life are under the guidance of the *Vedas*.

Vyasadeva–the original compiler of the *Vedas* and *Puranas*, and author of the *Vedanta-sutra* and *Mahabharata*.

Yajna–a Vedic ceremony.

Yoga–various processes of spiritual realization, all ultimately meant for attaining the Supreme Personality of Godhead.

Yoga-sutras–a classical text on yoga philosophy and practice, attributed to Patanjali.

Yogi–one who is striving in one of the Yoga processes.

Yukta-vairagya–real renunciation, in which one utilizes everything in the service of the Supreme.

About the Author

Vaiśeṣika Dasa is a renowned spiritual guide, known for his writings and lectures in which he gives practical advice about how to live a balanced life. He has been studying the *Bhagavad-gita* and the process of bhakti yoga for most of his life. As a teen, he was an avid spiritual seeker, and in 1973, at the age of sixteen, with his parents' blessings, he left high school to become a full-time monk dedicated to the practice of bhakti yoga and began his tutelage under his spiritual teacher, Srila A. C. Bhaktivedanta Swami Prabhupada.

After thirteen years living in ashramas, Vaiśeṣika transitioned to married life, wedding Nirakula Devi Dasi, also a disciple of Srila Prabhupada and a serious bhakti yoga practitioner. Together they have developed successful businesses and preside over a bhakti community of over four hundred families in northern California (ISKCON of Silicon Valley).

Vaiśeṣika travels worldwide sharing the knowledge he's gained from five decades of bhakti yoga practice integrated with his university studies, interactions with people from various cultures, and his calling as an entrepreneur. Speaking to youth groups and to audiences in corporations, universities, and nonprofits, he teaches universal principles of personal spiritual development and is recognized for making ancient yoga philosophy accessible and practical.

Stay Connected

I would love to hear your feedback or questions.

Vaiśeṣika Dāsa

thefourquestionsbook.com